COLOMBIANA

A Rediscovery of Recipes & Rituals
from the Soul of Colombia

Mariana Velásquez

HARPER

An Imprint of HarperCollinsPublishers

COLOMBIANA

HarperCollins books may be purchased for educational, business, or sales promotional use. For information, please email the Special Markets Department at SPsales@harpercollins.com.

Biblioteca Pública Piloto de Medellín has granted permission to reprint the following archival photographs. Page vi: *Vendedora de frutas* (Francisco Mejía, 1899–1979); page 4: *Cartagena* (Gabriel Carvajal Pérez, 1916–2008); page 53: *Barequera* (León Francisco Ruiz Flórez, 1933–); page 62: *Cartagena* (Andrés María Ripol, Padre); page 67: *Dolores Echavarría* (Fotografía Rodríguez, 1889–1995); page 105: *Río Cauca* (León Francisco Ruiz Flórez); pages 134–35: *Cultivo de café* (Gabriel Carvajal Pérez); page 194: *Boyacá* (Gabriel Carvajal Pérez); page 227: *Barranquilla* (Gabriel Carvajal Pérez); page 236: *Indias Wayúu* (León Francisco Ruiz Flórez); page 278: *Turbo* (Gabriel Carvajal Pérez).

FIRST EDITION

Designed by *Leah Carlson-Stanisic*

Photography by *Gentl & Hyers*

Illustrated by *Paulina Carrizosa*

Library of Congress Cataloging-in-Publication Data has been applied for.

ISBN 978-0-06-301943-0

24 25 RRDA 10 9 8 7 6 5 4 3

A Diego

Mi corazón de melocotón

CONTENTS

FROM BOGOTÁ
TO BIG SUR

My story starts on New Year's Eve in 1999, when I was working at my first cooking job in America. I was eighteen years old, and my mother, back in Bogotá, wanted me to be anything but a cook—despite the fact that she herself had devoted a life and career to the art of the table, curating and selling fine china and crystal. As I stood in a kitchen on the California coast, the new millennium was mere minutes away. The Post Ranch Inn, which sits atop Big Sur's breathtaking cliffs, is home to the award-winning restaurant Sierra Mar, where a party of sixty swayed outside, poised to ring in the New Year. I was in the kitchen, part of a thirteen-member crew cooking up a storm. More precisely, we were preparing a decadent, twelve-course dinner to be served in the exquisite dining room overlooking the Pacific Ocean, with linen table-cloths, gigantic freshly cut pink and white dahlias, and handmade dining ware. That night, still sweaty and watching the guests from afar, I toasted the year 2000 with a loving crew fresh from the kitchen's red-hot, tired line.

After I'd been peeling carrots, systematically, tirelessly, for days on end, the restaurant's then executive chef, Craig Von Foerster, a stocky, bald man with a tender smile, asked me to make the *mise en place* for the caviar with eggs and potatoes. I opted to cook the eggs and potatoes at the same time in one pot, just like my grandmother had always done at home. Chef Craig walked by the sixteen-burner gas stove and stopped abruptly upon glancing at my work. "Who did *this*?!" he yelled. It turns out that you're not supposed to cook eggs and potatoes in the same pot in a professional kitchen.

I identified myself, expecting dragon-fire to rain upon me. But then Chef turned around and spoke to me, almost in a murmur, "Never stop doing it this way. This is how you become a unique cook."

Even now, after being in New York City for more than half my life, the recipes and foods I grew up with continue to be at the core of my identity as a cook. My unapologetic "Colombianity" comes through in my accent, my organic approach to plating food, and the ruffles of my dresses. It shows when I make coconut fish *sancocho* for friends in the West Village on any given winter night, or shape up arepas on Thanksgiving morning for everyone before the true preparation for the feast begins. It is no coincidence that Diego, my Bogotánian husband, shares playlists that start with smooth tones but slowly make our guests dance a little in their seats—sometimes a lot.

My experience in restaurant kitchens was grounding to say the least. Working under chefs like Colombia's Harry Sasson and Prune's Gabrielle Hamilton in New York, among others, I learned discipline and hard work. Then, driven to explore my fixations with history and art beyond the kitchen line, I transitioned to the world of food magazines at publications like *Saveur* and *Eating Well*. There I learned the method and the minutiae that go into making a recipe trustworthy. I was constantly testing, developing, and researching every step. I remember taking the subway to Jackson Heights to buy a whole kid goat from a halal butcher, twice, to test and retest a biryani for a Pakistani story. That very dish was photographed by

Brooke Slezak, who told me I had a hand for food styling. "Food styling?" I replied. I had no idea that was something you could do for a living. And so it happened. Beauty, photography, storytelling, culture, and food. I realized I could preserve, forever into an image, a moment as ephemeral as a meal.

Since then, I've had the good fortune to work on many authors' cookbooks. I've had the honor of preparing and styling the food they had envisioned, written about, and tested. Now, after twenty years, I feel I've come full circle. I'm ready to write, style, and art direct my own vision.

Being both a Colombian cook and a food stylist in New York has inevitably shaped my cuisine. I constantly weave a fabric influenced by both cultures: their colors, exuberance, maximalism, history, mysticism, and politics. Everything comes together to create a food flavor and style all my own.

Yet, at my core, I am and will always be a Colombiana. No matter how much I enjoy tossing up a *frégola sarda* with pistachios and Pecorino Romano, or how regularly I braise lamb with olives and preserved lemons for the tagine I learned while working in Marrakesh, my country always remains my muse, my center, my compass.

And so here, finally, I offer you my sincere take on the Colombiana way of being. Creating and relishing intense yet balanced flavors, with my country as my muse, embracing the beauty and bounty of nature, celebrating with friends and family, and honoring the traditions that define a home.

COLOMBIANA

LA COCINA

COLOMBIAN CULTURE, CUISINE, PANTRY

To understand the food of my country, you must travel it by car, exploring every region and tasting your way through the mountains, valleys, fog forests, and markets. You could start by saying that our cuisine is a hearty mix of Indigenous, African, and European cultures. But truly defining the cuisine of Colombia in one phrase would be impossible, mainly because Colombia is one of the most biodiverse countries on earth by area, second only to Brazil. Imagine the range of dishes that can come from an almost countless variety of fruits, vegetables, tubers, and meats, all found within an area roughly twice the size of Texas. All climates, all year long. It's as challenging to define as it is delicious in its complexity.

And yet, there are three foods that serve as a unifying factor for all Colombians: arepas, empanadas, and the one-pot meal. This may sound like a vast simplification, but we have to start somewhere.

Arepas are grilled cakes with a dough made of white cornmeal, water, and salt. Unlike the way they are often served in America, where they may be stuffed with a variety of fillings, Colombians typically eat them plain, or maybe sprinkled with some fresh cheese. You could say our take on the arepa is distinctly minimalist.

In contrast, empanadas are filled with regional ingredients. They come in all sizes, made from different doughs, and, unlike their Argentinian counterparts, they are mostly deep fried. You'll find crispy dough stuffed with braised rabbit and vegetables in the foothills of La Sierra Nevada, potatoes and egg in the Andes Mountains, and *pipián* (pumpkin seeds or peanuts) filling along the Venezuelan border, to name just a few.

The third food that unites us all, the one-pot soup or stew, has endless variations. On the northern coast they make a coconut-based soup with fish, corn, potatoes, yams, and spices called sancocho, which comes from the Spanish verb *sancochar* ("to parboil"). In the valley of the Cauca River, they have *sancocho valluno*, a flavorful soup made by slowly cooking chicken, beef ribs, plantains, yuca, and potatoes, served with avocados, rice, and a good squeeze of lime. On the western branch of the Andes, there is an elaborate stew named *mute* that contains chickpeas, corn, beef shank, potatoes, and even pasta. But in the Antioquian region at the center of the country, the one-pot meal changes dramatically. Instead of fish, you'll find pigs' feet; instead of a tomato stew, there's a red bean soup accompanied by sweet plantains, white rice, and powdered brisket; its name: *frijolada*. Up in the Andes where it's cold, the protein is chicken, and the stew is creamy and made with capers and a *Galinsoga parviflora* herb we call *guasca*. This variation usually includes three types of potatoes. It's called *ajiáco*. From the *mazamorra chiquita* of Boyacá to the *puchero santafereño* of Bogotá, these earnest and humble preparations are undoubtedly the core of our cuisine.

Another food important to Colombia is the *tamal*, a meal packaged in tightly wrapped leaves that Mexican cooks have internationalized. It generally encompasses a starch, a protein, a grain, seasonings, and some veggies. In Santander, a Colombian region in the east near Venezuela, tamales are filled with chickpeas, corn, and pork belly and wrapped in plantain leaves. In the steamy region of Tolima they are made with rice, chicken, and a hard-boiled egg. There could be an entire book written about their varieties: pasteles, tamales, *bollos,* and *envueltos.* (Maybe I'll address these in my next endeavor!)

Since Colombian food isn't spicy, most of the dishes I mention here are topped with *ají:* a green salsa made of scallions, cilantro, vinegar, and small green chilis. *Ají* is to Colombians what sriracha is to Californians—we add it to everything, adjusting to personal taste and spice tolerance.

Colombians also have an indisputable sweet tooth—myself included! From simple stacked guava paste slices with fresh cheese slivers to *arequipe* (our version of dulce de leche) to rich coconut custards, tropical fruit confitures, and marmalades and jams, we celebrate the richness and abundance of the land. Colombian desserts come in all shapes and forms. Cake rolls, ice creams, flans, meringues, and cookies. You'll find creamy and fruity ice cream bars filling portable coolers on streets across the entire country, from Pasto in the south to Barranquilla in the north, and yes, even Queens in New York City.

We're also known to party. You can fact check me on this, but I understand that Colombia has more festivities and festivals than weekends in a year. For instance, the International Tournament of Improvised Verse Duels in the city of Yopal, the Green Moon Festival in the San Andrés islands, and the Pineapple Fair in the town of Lebrija. Our special occasions are usually accompanied by a drink. The king of them all is the distilled sugarcane liquor called *aguardiente,* which literally means "fire water." There are also any number of delicious, homemade beverages and spirits: *chicha, masato, guarapo, mistela,* and *chirrinchi* are all fermented, preserved, and sometimes aged, made with grains, roots, fruits, and seeds. See page 225 for my take on almond rice *chicha.*

I am not a culinary history expert, but I do believe that Colombia's cuisine is dictated by the flavors, traditions, and influences of its regions. Yet the philosophy of Colombian food could boil down to one concept that I personally love: More is more. If there is room for ten at a traditional *sancocho* lunch, there sure is room for twelve. There are always several side dishes, not one but maybe two desserts, flowers come in baskets, textiles and jars of ají dress our tables. In Colombia, generosity isn't a noun, it's a verb full of warmth. I see it in the abundance of carnations and anthuriums, chilled *aguardiente,* bowls filled with pineapples, *granadillas,* and ripe papayas and a maximalist aesthetic that, while kitschy at times, makes our tables and our meals a one-of-a-kind experience.

COLOMBIANAS

There are more than twenty-three million of us Colombian women. Together, we make up an undefinable mix of heritage, culture, and backgrounds. But while our struggles and inspirations vary by region and personal experience, I believe we share a core value: No matter the status, capacity, or budget, if you show up at our door, Colombianas will offer to feed you. Being generous with food is in our spirit.

It would be an understatement to say that Colombian women have struggled over the centuries. Our country had been mired in divisiveness and political conflict almost since its inception. I still remember reading about Policarpa Salavarrieta, who spied for the revolutionary forces in the early nineteenth century. She participated in Colombia's independence when she was only fourteen years old. The National Colombian Women's holiday is celebrated on the anniversary of her death. Time scarred the country with decades of violence, internal war, drug trafficking, and displacement. I think this pushed Colombianas to raise their families with true grit and resilience. Today, four out of every ten adult women in Colombia are heads of their own households, which means they have one or more mouths to feed every day with no partner or financial support.

Hardship has increased our capacity for creativity and inventiveness when feeding our loved ones. For instance, in the city of Popayán, I witnessed local women make *carantánta*—a salty snack made with the leftover cracklings that stick to the sides of metal pots where corn is cooked over an open fire. I learned that this method comes from the need to utilize every bit of food and stretch every ingredient as far as it can go. Nothing goes to waste and, in cases like this, parchment-thin corn becomes an unexpected delicacy.

I learned to cook fish wrapped in *bijao* leaves over an open fire right in the heart of San Basilio de Palenque, the first-ever free African town (built by former slaves) in all of the Americas, located two hours inland from the Atlantic coast. There are Afro-Colombian communities like this all over Colombia, and they are among the most vulnerable populations of the country, particularly the working women. These communities have been subject to not only a history of violence and conflict in their regions but they also continue to suffer from systemic inequities such as lack of access to potable water and basic needs like paved roads and schools. Yet, they have managed to persevere, creating a rich and flavorful cuisine by using native ingredients and preserving heirloom cooking techniques.

In Santa Cruz de Mompox, a town on the banks of the Magdalena River, I listened to the stories that defined this town with a long history of music, craftsmanship, and traditions. Doña Ada, a seventy-two-year-old woman who has spent her entire life in the village, shared with me a quote from Colombia's liberator, Simón Bolívar: "If to Caracas I owe my life, then to Mompox I owe my glory." Doña Ada has watched the decades unfold from behind her stove, candying lime peels for her famous Dulce de Limón, which has been sold for years through the same green colonial window with a handwritten sign that reads "Hay Dulce de Limón," meaning "Yes, we have Lime Dessert."

Our resilience is also palpable in the Wayuu women who inhabit La Guajira's deep desert. The women walk for miles to gather water, forage for cactus fruit, and harvest sea salt from the open-air mines in small towns like Manaure, whose sole existence is dependent on the mine itself. While researching their traditional cooking techniques, specific to the country's northern peninsula, I had the honor of learning how the Wayuu women prepare their *friche*, a stew of goat meat and blood, and *chicha*, a fermented beverage made with rice or corn.

But it was the women in my family who profoundly and consistently shaped my culinary heritage more than anyone else. Like most upper-middle-class families in Bogotá during the 1980s, we had a live-in nanny and cook, who was and still is an integral part of the family. That's why Alfonso Cuarón's 2018 film *Roma* resonated so much with audiences worldwide, myself included. In my case, it was Teresa, now eighty-two years old, from El Guavio, Cundinamarca, who lived with us for more than twenty years until retirement.

One night, when I was twelve, Teresa indulged me by letting me make dinner for my family from a recipe I found in a book. She sat with me way past my bedtime while I waited for cakes to come out of the oven and taught me how to make soups and mix dressings by shaking the ingredients together in a jar. Teresa was patient, abiding, and truthful—just like the flavors of her cooking. I pay tribute to her as well as to Lorena, Lola, Euge, Rosa, Teodolinda, Dolores, Anita, Ofelia, and Dora—the women who took care of my extended family and those around us. They, our caretakers, with their patience, love, and incredible cooking skills, helped raise entire generations at the expense of being away from their own families and children. Our universes became entangled at times, but that invisible social barrier was palpable. I never noticed it until I left my country. Only from the outside I can see how these women devoted their lives to the service of privileged families like my own.

Then there is my mother, Carmiña Villegas, a fabulous cook and host extraordinaire. A self-made entrepreneur with an eye for beauty, exquisite taste, and a vision for business, she became a household name in all things table decor across the country. Persistence, determination, and the right way to set an impeccable table are the most significant lessons I learned from her. To this day, I carry them in my mind and in my heart.

Both my grandmothers were truly my gateway to the kitchen. My grandmother Adela, of German descent, whom I always called Tia Lilita, would teach me to bake *pan de yucas* (yuca cheese bread) in a clay oven at her ranch in the eastern flatlands. My grandmother Lurys, a first-generation Lebanese whom everyone called Lola, taught all her granddaughters how to shape perfect zeppelin kibbes from a young age. Growing up in an urban setting in Bogotá gave me access to international foods; but it was all those vacations in the countryside, visiting farms, roadside stands, and rural kitchens, where I truly began to experience traditional Colombian foods and cooking techniques like homemade fruit vinegars, wood fire cooking, and ancestral earth ovens, among many others.

Once I moved to the US, my mentors were mostly women as well. Quickly, I understood my responsibility as an immigrant to preserve an untouched *Colombianity* within myself. While taking heed that my heritage didn't disappear entirely, I adopted many freeing elements of American culture. I became less preoccupied with pleasing my family with my career choices. I took the risk to embark on an unusual profession. It was in this country where I felt I could openly and honestly be whoever I wanted to be.

So many other Colombian women I've connected with over the years—those who migrated to Madrid, Manila, Hong Kong, Shanghai, or Queens, New York—all continue to crave and prepare the flavors from home, no matter where they are. Each and every one of them has a story and a unique set of personal circumstances, but I am pretty sure they have all, at least once, packed a jar of *arequipe* or a bag of coffee into their suitcases.

South America

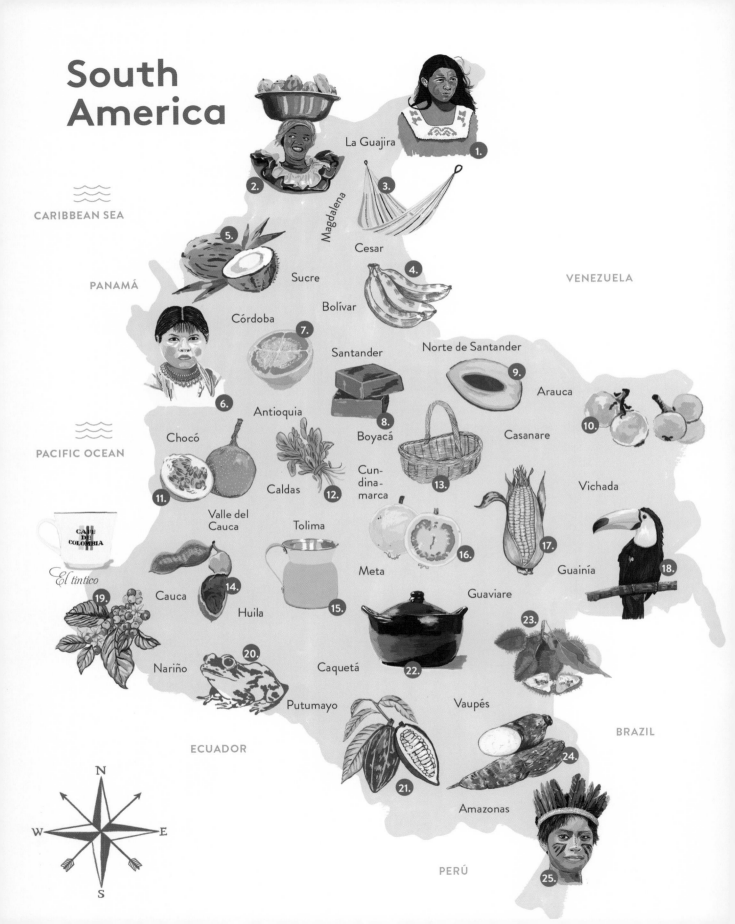

CARIBBEAN SEA

PANAMÁ

PACIFIC OCEAN

VENEZUELA

BRAZIL

ECUADOR

PERÚ

La Guajira

Magdalena

Cesar

Sucre

Bolívar

Córdoba

Norte de Santander

Santander

Arauca

Casanare

Boyacá

Antioquia

Chocó

Cundi-
na-
marca

Vichada

Caldas

Valle del
Cauca

Tolima

Meta

Guainía

Cauca

Huila

Guaviare

El tintico

CAFÉ
DE
COLOMBIA

Nariño

Caquetá

Vaupés

Putumayo

Amazonas

N

W   E

S

COLOMBIA IS DIVIDED INTO 6 NATURAL REGIONS:

Amazonia, Andina, Caribe, Insular, Orinoquía, and Pacífico. The country has the second-highest biodiversity in the world, behind Brazil.

The territory is divided into 32 states. Colombia hosts about 10 percent of the planet's biodiversity and worldwide, it ranks first in bird and orchid species diversity and second in plants, butterflies, freshwater fish, and amphibians.

1. **INDÍGENA Wayuu**

2. **PALENQUERA**

3. **HAMMOCK**

4. **BANANAS**

5. **COCONUT**

6. **INDÍGENA EMBERA**

7. **LULO**

8. **PANELA**

9. **MAMEY**

10. **NÍSPERO**

11. **GRANADILLA**

12. **GUASCAS**

13. **BASKET** Talented artisans work with with natural fibers and textiles across the regions

14. **TAMARIND**

15. **POT for hot chocolate**

16. **GUAVA**

17. **CORN**

18. **TOUCAN** More than 1,900 reported bird species in the country

19. **COFFEE**

20. **FROG** There are 749 species

21. **CACAO**

22. **CHAMBA CERAMIC TERRINE**

23. **ACHIOTE in flower**

24. **YUCA**

25. **INDÍGENA of the Amazonia**
There are at least 26 indigenous ethnic groups in Colombia's Amazonia region

LA DESPENSA

THE PANTRY

ACHIOTE OR ANNATTO

What is it?	A crimson red spice made of annatto seeds that comes from the flowering pods of an evergreen shrub. You can find it ground into a powder or as a paste.
Flavor Profile	Nutty, sweet, earthy.
Uses	As a seasoning and color in stews, soups, and all sorts of empanada and tamal fillings.
Good Substitute	Sweet paprika.
Favorite Brands and Good Sources	Look for it in the Latin American or Mexican section of grocery stores. You'll find it in seeds or ground form.

AGUARDIENTE

What is it?	The name of this national liqueur of Colombia translates to "burning water," or "fire water." Made from distilled sugarcane and anise, it is prepared with pride. Many estates and provinces are aguardiente producers, and its qualities and national origin are defended by locals with the same fervor as their local *fútbol* team.
Flavor Profile	Very strong (60% proof), licorice-scented.
Uses	Mostly consumed as an *aperitivo*, chilled in shot glasses or sipped on the rocks with lime. Aguardiente is also used in cooking and baking.
Good Substitute	Raki, ouzo, or Pernod.
Favorite Brands and Good Sources	Liquor stores with a wide range of international drinks will most often carry aguardiente. My personal favorite is Aguardiente Antioqueño.

CANNED COCONUT MILK

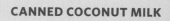

What is it?	Grated coconut processed with some liquid to extract all of its fat, flavor, and liquid, then stabilized with guar gum (a stabilizer made from beans).
Flavor Profile	Rich and creamy and nutty.
Uses	Soups, stews, rices, and desserts.
Good Substitute:	None.
Favorite Brands and Good Sources	The kind used for cooking comes canned, and there are different varieties to choose from: full-fat, lite, coconut cream, and sweetened (never purchase sweetened unless making piña coladas on a whim!). I prefer Thai coconut milk and call for lite or full-fat, depending on the recipe. What makes Thai coconut milk better than others is the fact that it doesn't break, it has a thick layer of cream on top, and it tastes fresh. It is easily found in the Asian section of the grocery store.

Note: In some regions of the United States there may be only one name brand available for Latin American products needed for several of the recipes in this book—mostly for beans, frozen fruit pulps, and seasonings. I chose to not name this brand.

CHICHARRÓN

What is it?	Pork cracklings, skins, or rinds are a popular snack and side dish in Colombia. One could say that there are two versions of *chicharrón*: The first is meaty pork cracklings made from the fresh skin of the pork belly (page 145), cooked by rendering or frying and usually served as part of a meal. The other version is a packaged snack frequently salted and flavored with lemon or spice—sort of like potato chips.
Flavor Profile	Meaty, crunchy, salty, and bold.
Uses	As an element of *fritanga* (a grand melange of sausages, chorizos, and charcuterie commonly served in many regions of the country). In *frijolada* (see page 142), coriander and orange buns (see page 198), and grilled corn salad (see page 241).
Good Substitute	Since its strongest contribution to a dish is crunch, you can replace *chicharrón* with salted yuca chips, potato chips, or your choice of crispy snack.
Favorite Brands and Good Sources	My favorite packaged brand available in the US is Epic—these are oven-baked pork rinds, which I prefer because they are meaty, dry, and not too fatty.

MASA HARINA, AREPA HARINA, MASECA

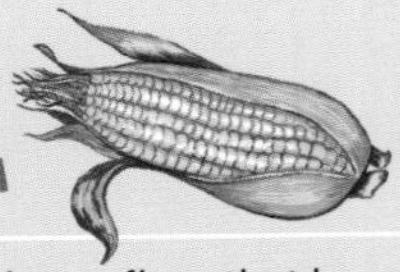

What is it?	Essentially this is a dried corn flour that has undergone the nixtamalization process, which involves soaking corn in slaked lime or wood ash for many hours, loosening the hulls from the kernels, and—in a much more chemically advanced way than I'm describing—softening the corn to make it workable into a dough. *Masa* means dough.
Flavor Profile	Looks like a fine cornmeal and it has a neutral, dried-corn taste.
Uses	Tamales, empanada dough, arepas, *bollos*, and porridges.
Good Substitute	If following a recipe, it is important to not replace with an equal amount of other flours, as the recipe most likely won't work.
Favorite Brands and Good Sources:	*Masa harina* is now widely available, and all you need to do to turn it into dough is add water. Masa comes in both white and yellow varieties. My favorite brand is Masienda—an artisanal masa made in Los Angeles that is widely available online. Also in your local supermarket you'll find P.A.N. and Bob's Red Mill Masa, which are of great quality.

PANELA

What is it?	Unrefined cane sugar is an essential ingredient in our cuisine and a staple in our daily life. One of the things that make panela unique and different from other unrefined sugars around the globe is that it is still mostly produced by hand in *trapiches*. After the sugarcane juice gets boiled down into a thick syrup, it is shaped into blocks, branded with the name of the maker, packaged in bundles of ninety-six units, wrapped in intertwined sugarcane leaves, and then tied together with a rope. Each package is then slipped into a burlap bag and sent off to the markets.
Flavor Profile	Sweet caramel with slightly bitter vanilla notes.

Uses	Panela is given to babies in bottles with milk, served as an infusion with lime to cure colds, and poured hot at roadside stands with chewy melted cheese (this one is bizarre, yet is one of my favorite things). Panela is used in traditional recipes like roasts and braises, and in desserts, beverages, and confitures.
Good Substitute	Coconut sugar, dark brown sugar, date sugar, or maple sugar. Other countries produce unrefined sugar like panela and it is referred to as *piloncillo*, Thai palm sugar, *chancaca*, and rapadura.
Favorite Brands and Good Sources	Panela can be found both in block form and as a powder in Latin American and Asian markets, as well as health food stores. You can also find panela at www.limonarium.com.

YUCA FLOUR (ALSO CALLED YUCA STARCH)

What is it?	A starchy flour made from yuca root (also called cassava, manioc, *manioca*, or casaba). This flour and its byproducts are essential to Brazilian cuisine and that of the Amazonian region in Colombia, Peru, and Ecuador.
Flavor Profile	A sweet, fine flour.
Uses	Both savory and sweet preparations such as *Pandebono* (page 110), *Tortica de Yuca, Coco y Toronja* (page 42), and *Enyucado* (page 272).
Good Substitute	For baked goods I wouldn't risk replacing in equal quantities, but in most cases sweet rice flour works well.
Favorite Brands and Good Sources:	Thanks to the gluten-free craze, yuca flour is widely available. Popular brands such as Bob's Red Mill are of great quality.

LÁCTEOS (DAIRY)

AREQUIPE

What is it?	Making *arequipe* from scratch can take up to three hours of stirring, as it is the result of cooking milk slowly with sugar and cinnamon until it reduces, browns, and turns into a decadent velvety caramel spread. The origin of this creamy caramel is debatable, but my favorite theory is that it was brought over from the Philippines via Acapulco in the infamous Galeón de Manila in the seventeenth century. See recipes for the long and the quick versions on page 271.
Flavor Profile	Sweet, creamy, caramel, and vanilla notes.
Uses	Can be eaten on its own by the spoonful or as a spread and ingredient in many, many Colombian desserts.
Good Substitute	*Cajeta, dulce de leche, manjar.*
Favorite Brands and Good Sources	For ready-made *arequipe* try Alpina (Colombian brand) and Stonewall Kitchen Dulce de Leche Sauce (US brand).

CUAJADA

What is it?	Made daily in the dairy regions of Colombia, *cuajada* is made from strained cheese curds from fresh milk. The cheese takes on the half-dome shape of the metal and plastic colanders used by artisans all over Colombia.
Flavor Profile	A mild soft cheese with a semi-firm texture. The texture of the cheese is pleasantly squeaky and soft.
Uses	A classic Colombian dessert is *cuajada con melao*: *cuajada* drizzled with panela syrup. Also, *cuajada* is one of the ingredients in traditional *almojábanas*.
Good Substitute	When it is used as an ingredient, 2% or 4% cottage cheese or fresh ricotta cheese works very well. As a dessert, farmer cheese or *fromage blanc* are great replacements.
Favorite Brands and Good Sources	May not be readily available in the United States—check the fresh section of the supermarket and Latin American stores or online.

QUESITO

What is it?	A fresh, soft, and crumbly cheese.
Flavor Profile	Mild, usually low in salt.
Uses	As a spread for arepas, in savory bread doughs and desserts, or alongside blackberry preserves.
Good Substitute	Similar to Mexican *queso fresco* or farmer cheese.
Favorite Brands and Good Sources	My favorite brand is La Finquita.

QUESO COSTEÑO

What is it?	A salted and crumbly cheese produced mostly in coastal cities by pressing milk curds with salt into a wooden box. It can be found either fresh or slightly aged.
Flavor Profile	Salty and firm, cuts well into cubes, and depending on how long it has been aged it can be either crumbly or chewy.
Uses	As a breakfast cheese with a side of boiled yuca—a match called *matrimonio* (matrimony). *Queso costeño* is also a key ingredient in *mote de queso* (see page 157) as well as fritters such as *buñuelos*.
Good Substitute	*Ricotta salata* or Mexican Cotija.
Favorite Brands and Good Sources	Aged cheese section of the supermarket and Latin American stores.

SUERO

What is it?	A preparation common in the states of Córdoba, Sucre, and Bolívar on the Caribbean coast made with fresh milk, an acid (lime juice or vinegar), and salt. An adaptation of *labneh*, brought over by Middle Eastern immigrants, *suero* is a dairy product that complements so many dishes of these particular regions. On dairy farms, *suero* is fermented in gourds, which gives it a unique flavor, and, in some cases, the top fat skin layer (known as the *nata*) is stirred in—this version is known as *atollabuey*, which literally means "a stuck ox."
Flavor Profile	Tangy, creamy, and salty.
Uses	As a spread for fritters such as egg arepas, *carimañolas* (see page 153), or *mote de queso* (see page 157); slathered over steamed or fried yuca and plantains.
Good Substitute	Similar to crème fraîche and Middle Eastern *labneh*. Another great option is to blend plain Greek yogurt with a squeeze of lime juice and a pinch of salt.
Favorite Brands and Good Sources	El Latino—sold online and in Latin American stores.

FRUTAS (FRUITS)

CURUBA

What is it?	This is one of the sixty-four known *Passiflora* species, oblong in shape and also known as banana passion fruit. Its vines are used to construct fences across the Andes and its beautiful flower is of a dark purple hue, and shaped like a lily.
Flavor Profile	Sweet with a touch of astringency.
Uses	Mostly fruit juice and mousses.
Good Substitute	None.
Favorite Brands and Good Sources	*Curuba* can be found in specialty stores and Latin American markets. Its frozen pulp made by the company La Fe is also a great option.

FEIJOA

What is it?	This small, oval-shaped, forest green fruit comes from the mountains of northern Uruguay, Brazil, Argentina, and Colombia. Its name comes from the Brazilian botanist João da Silva Feijó.
Flavor Profile	Slightly astringent, a bit sandy; has a floral aroma and meaty consistency.
Uses	Commonly used for liqueurs, ciders, and even wine. It is also a favorite fruit in ice creams and desserts in the mountain regions.
Good Substitute	None.
Favorite Brands and Good Sources	*Feijoa* is difficult to find in the US.

GRANADILLA

What is it?	Also known as *grenadia*, or sugar fruit, this fruit has been growing in the Andes since 1200 BC. A supersweet pulp that keeps its multiple seeds united into one gooey sac inside a gourd.
Flavor Profile	Delicate, sweet, and seedy.
Uses	It's mostly eaten fresh.
Good Substitute	None.
Favorite Brands and Good Sources	Find it on your next trip to Colombia or Peru!

GUANÁBANA (SOURSOP)

What is it?	The Mexican music icon Chavela Vargas once used this fruit to describe her lover's lips. She said, "Your mouth, a ripe *guanábana* blessing." A blessing indeed, this fruit has more than 150 identified varieties, but most of them have the same structure: a crocodile green outer skin with a surprisingly white, pillowy pulp encasing a shiny black, round pit.
Flavor Profile	Wonderfully creamy, sweet, and a tiny bit sour.
Uses	Perfect base for custards—mixed with cream and a touch of sugar it becomes a filling for the classic *merengón*, a meringue dessert made with cream and fresh fruit (see page 128).
Good Substitute	Chirimoyas, custard apples, or frozen pulp.
Favorite Brands and Good Sources	Frozen pulp by La Fe, and *guanábana* pulp preserved in syrup is sold by Mountain brand.

GUAYABA (GUAVA)

What is it?	Known in Colombia as *guayaba*, this fruit has five times the vitamin C of an orange but is not a member of the citrus family. Fabulously sweet, *guayabas* are the main ingredient in many Colombian fruit leathers, jams, and pastes.
Flavor Profile	Sweet and meaty.
Uses	When in harvest, its trees are so prolific that local makers had to invent multiple types of pastries and sweets so that the fruit wouldn't go to waste. Still, they sometimes can't keep up. It is also used as a dessert bite with *arequipe*. The wood from the guava tree is often used for smoking meats and fish, and is sometimes even used as medicine.
Good Substitute	Quince paste.
Favorite Brands and Good Sources	Guavas come fresh in clamshell boxes, as a paste cut into squares, and in jelly form. Iberia brand is sold at Target and other major supermarkets.

LULO

What is it?	Also known as *naranjilla*, this is a round, ochre fruit with a rubbery and fussy outer skin and a dark green, soft, jelly-like flesh.
Flavor Profile	Both sour and sweet, sometimes described as green apple or lime.
Uses	Beverages such as *lulada* (see page 107); popsicles; fruit fillings for truffles, pies, and tarts.
Good Substitute	None.
Favorite Brands and Good Sources	La Fe makes a fantastic frozen pulp, which I recommend using as a replacement for the whole fruit.

MAMEY

What is it?	Also known as sapote, mamey is the fruit of an evergreen tree originally from southern Mexico. The word *sapote* comes from the Aztec *tzapotl*. The brown, oblong, leathery skin encases a creamy reddish flesh that can be eaten with a spoon.
Flavor Profile	Some describe its flavor as a combination of roasted sweet potato, avocado, and banana.
Uses	Smoothies, pies, preserves, and as fresh fruit.
Good Substitute	Ripe persimmons, sweet potatoes, or very ripe papayas.
Favorite Brands and Good Sources	Sold online by several suppliers and in the produce section of Asian and Latin American supermarkets.

MARACUYÁ (PASSION FRUIT)

What is it?	A canary yellow fruit the size of a tennis ball that encases a bundle of sour and sweet seeds so juicy that its nectar will run down your elbow when you crack one open. This fruit's name comes from the Catholic missionaries that discovered it during colonial times: the Passion of the Christ.
Flavor Profile	Sour, floral, and very juicy.
Uses	Ice cream, juices, sauces, and desserts.
Good Substitute	The *gulupa*, also from the *Passiflora* family, is smaller, with a deep purple color, and a little sweeter than its Colombian counterpart. Wrinkled skin is a good sign that a *gulupa* or passion fruit is ripe.
Favorite Brands and Good Sources	In the US, it is usually easier to find the *maracuyá*'s cousin, the *gulupa*. Look for frozen pulp with no additives or frozen concentrate.

NÍSPERO

What is it?	In Spanish, this fruit is also referred to as *sapodilla*. In English, you can find it as loquat. A light brown, rough outer skin reveals the most exquisite peachy flesh with a soft orange, coral hue.
Flavor Profile	Similar to cantaloupe, but with a grainier texture and a sweet, nutty taste.
Uses	Commonly used in marmalades and smoothies.
Good Substitute	None.
Favorite Brands and Good Sources	Sold online and in frozen pulp form in Latin American and Asian markets.

TOMATE DE ÁRBOL

What is it?	This egg-shaped fruit isn't a tomato, yet we call it such, and like tomatoes, it can be yellow or red. *Tomate de árbol* grows on a tree and is also known as *tamarillo* in New Zealand, Sri Lanka, and South Africa.
Flavor Profile	Umami, sour, and a touch of sweet.
Uses	It's often pickled or consumed in juice form. Perfect to make sauces and jams.
Good Substitute	Ripe plum tomatoes with lime juice.
Favorite Brands and Good Sources	Sold whole frozen and preserved in syrup in Latin American markets or online.

UCHUVA

What is it?	A beautiful golden fruit wrapped in a husk—imagine a mini orange tomatillo.
Flavor Profile	Savory, sweet, with an acidic taste and a meaty texture. Referred to as the "umami" berry.
Uses	Salads, pastry decorations, preserves, and a wide range of desserts.
Good Substitute	Small yellow plums, yellow cherry tomatoes.
Favorite Brands and Good Sources	This fruit is imported to the US by brands like Ocati, and sold all over the world at specialty stores. It's similar to the American-grown cape gooseberry or husk cherry, which can be found at farmers' markets toward the end of summer. Colombia produces and exports so many *uchuvas* that innovators have developed disposable dinnerware from recycled husks.

VERDURAS Y TUBÉRCULOS (PRODUCE)

CILANTRO

What is it?	Native to Europe and brought by the Spaniards to Mexico in the 1500s, cilantro, also known as Mexican parsley, plays a paramount role in Colombian cooking—its stems, leaves, and flowers are all utilized. There are many varieties of cilantro, but, for our purposes, any will do. The dried seeds of the cilantro plant, known as coriander, are used as a seasoning, either ground or whole, in recipes like empanada fillings (see page 180) and jam (see page 139).
Flavor Profile	Fresh, citrusy, and a bit tangy to some and to others, cilantro, sadly, tastes like soap. Some studies show that this taste experience is genetic.
Uses	Soups, salads, ají, stews, and fillings. Cilantro leaves are also sprinkled over ceviche.
Good Substitute	Flat-leaf or Italian parsley.
Favorite Brands and Good Sources	In Asian and Latin American markets, sometimes you'll find flowering cilantro that has frilly leaves and longer stems, as opposed to the scalloped three-petal leaves more commonly found in supermarkets across the United States.
Insight:	To preserve cilantro, wash, spin dry, and keep in a sealed container or bag in the refrigerator, away from the coldest temperatures, to prevent browning.

ÑAME

What is it?	Also known as white yam, this brown, knobby medium-size tuber is cultivated in Asia, Africa, South America, and Australia.
Flavor Profile	Starchy, creamy, with woody notes.
Uses	Usually stewed or made into soups, it makes an appearance in the form of a creamy soup with cheese in my *mote de queso* (see page 157).
Good Substitute	Equal parts yuca and peeled russet potatoes.
Favorite Brands and Good Sources	*Ñame* can be easily found in Asian and Latin American markets.

PAPAS CRIOLLAS (CRIOLLA POTATOES)

What is it?	A tiny yellow potato that grows in the high-altitude valleys of Colombia, Peru, and Bolivia.
Flavor Profile	Sweet and creamy.
Uses	It is one of the three potato varieties used in *ajiáco* (see page 126), served fried alongside grilled meats, and in vegetable soups.
Good Substitute:	Gold creamer potatoes.
Favorite Brands and Good Sources	Can be found whole, frozen in specialty stores around the country.

PLÁTANOS (PLANTAINS)

What is it?	*Musa x paradisiaca* is the Linnean name given to the plantain and banana plant. How can one not be enchanted by this name? I am. Plantains surely are one of the muses of Colombian cooking, especially because of the way their flavor transforms as they ripen. Young plantains are very green, almost gray, but slowly, as they ripen and turn yellow and darker, they grow sweeter. Colombian cooking utilizes plantains at varying stages of ripeness.
Flavor Profile	Taste ranges depending on ripeness. Green plantains are starchy and savory; when they are very ripe they are almost black and they become sweet and sticky.
Uses	Green plantains work very well in *sancocho* (see page 111) or thinly sliced into coins and deep-fried. When they are *pintón*, which means when they begin to show a bit of yellow, it makes the ideal addition to an eggplant puree called *boronía* or as *patacones* (see page 171). There are recipes that call for ultra-ripe plantains, which are completely black, and all they need is heat; cooking them on the back of the grill while the whole asado is made transforms this fruit into candy. On the side of the road in Palomino by La Sierra Nevada—a tiny magical town with ancestry and energy of the local wise Kogi community—one can get honey-sweet, fire-roasted plantains, split open lengthwise and stuffed with fresh cheese and guava paste—mind you, right from your car window.
Good Substitute	None.
Favorite Brands and Good Sources	Most supermarkets now carry plantains.
Insight	Oddly enough, green plantains will tend to oxidize (blacken) when cut with a knife. A native technique is to break green plantains into chunks with the side of your thumb—however, that can be quite hard on your nail. A technique I learned by watching women make soups is to use a teaspoon to essentially take chunks off the plantain until there is nothing left.

POLEO

What is it?	An aromatic herb from the mint family, also called squaw mint or pudding grass.
Flavor Profile	Fresh, fragrant, with tones of bitterness that add depth.
Uses	Soups, rice recipes, and fillings. Traditionally used in the Chocó region on the Pacific coast.
Good Substitute	Spearmint or peppermint.

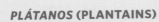

YUCA

What is it?	Yuca is a long, brown, starchy root grown in Latin America. Yuca may also be called cassava, manioc, or tapioca, among other names.
Flavor Profile	Plain and fibrous carbohydrate with a slight tang.
Uses	It is prepared like a potato: fried, pureed, stewed, boiled, and roasted. It is very versatile and is at its prime when it is snow white on the inside. If it has dark lines on the inside, it will be bitter.
Good Substitute	Peeled russet potatoes when called for in soups.

Favorite Brands and Good Sources	Buying yuca is tricky because you don't know if it's good until you crack it open. Thankfully, it is quite inexpensive, so it's a good idea to buy a bit more than you need. Yuca keeps very well with onions and potatoes in a dark, dry place. A fabulous alternative is frozen yuca: already peeled and guaranteed to be sweet. Fresh and frozen yuca is readily available in supermarkets and Latin American stores.

UTENSILS

CALDERO (CAULDRON)

What is it?	This is "the workhorse of any Hispanic kitchen," as its most common maker, IMUSA, describes it. A cast-aluminum pot is to Colombian households what a wok is to Chinese cooking. Essential to cooking rice, simmering stews, and frying, this is one of those cooking tools that also holds an emotional attachment. The *caldero* tells the tale… It's ever present and often outlives every pot in the kitchen and it comes in all sizes.
Uses	Rice, stews, soups, and braises. Invented in 1935 in the Antioquia region, it is still exclusively produced in Colombia. The *caldero*'s durability makes it unlike any other cooking vessel I've ever used.
Good Substitute	The Duchess by Great Jones and Le Creuset 5.5 quart Dutch Oven
Favorite Brands and Good Sources	Online from IMUSA or in the kitchenware section of Latin American markets.

CHOCOLATERA

What is it?	A stainless-steel pitcher primarily used to make hot chocolate; its wide bottom allows for vigorous whisking without milk spilling all over. These chocolate pitchers last a lifetime and only get better with age.
Uses	Hot chocolate (see page 52), *agua de panela*, warming up broths and milk.
Good Substitute	Tall narrow saucepan.
Favorite Brands and Good Sources	Online.

MOLINILLO

What is it?	This wooden chocolate whisk also serves as a frother and stirrer to make a foamy delight out of every hot chocolate.
Uses	Beverage preparation such as *patillazo* (see page 218), hot chocolate (see page 52), and *lulada* (see page 107).
Good Substitute	A milk frother or a large wooden spoon or wooden muddle.
Favorite Brands and Good Sources	Online from Plaza Bolivar.

PARRILLA PARA AREPAS (AREPA GRILL)

What is it?	This is a round metal rack used to grill arepas over low heat over the burner. In Colombia, each household owns two or three. They're very inexpensive and easy to clean. If you love arepas, you must own one.
Uses	Reheating arepas and toast.
Good Substitute	Cast-iron skillet or ceramic *tiesto*.
Favorite Brands and Good Sources	Online from IMUSA and in the kitchenware section of Latin American markets.

TIESTO

What is it?	A clay cured platter used for cooking over an open flame.
Uses	Useful for charring vegetables and heating arepas.
Good Substitute	Cast-iron skillet.
Favorite Brands and Good Sources	Online from Plaza Bolivar.

ON NATURAL PACKAGING AND LEAVES

In my obsession with sustainable packaging for groceries and food, I found myself diving into an academic study from Colombia's Ministry of Culture (published in the 1970s) about the use of leaves and husks to package, preserve, transport, and sell food across different regions of the country.

It turns out that in the early 1920s, around the gold mining areas of Antioquia, salt was packaged in tightly sealed leaf bundles. They used a leaf from the *bijao* plant, which is a bit wider than the commonly known monstera plant leaves. Ferns would also be used to nestle raw meat into wooden boxes from the slaughterhouse to the market. Raw eggs were carefully cradled and cushioned by corn husks and then tied together with rope. This was the way to keep them intact through horseback journeys. Plastic wrap has now replaced these natural tools in an infuriating, unsustainable, tragic loss of craftsmanship.

Yet, some of the foods of Colombia continue to be wrapped in natural packaging, including *bollos* (page 49), panela, cheeses, tamales, and the ever-sweet *bocadillos veleños*. This organic aesthetic inspires me to use natural fibers such as corn husks, plantain leaves, and rope to wrap gifts, decorate tables, and incorporate as props in my food styling work.

IN THE MORNING

EN LA MAÑANA

Beginning the day with a proper ritual brings my body and soul into harmony. This is why breakfast holds an undeniably sacred space in our Williamsburg, Brooklyn, home, where I dream up dishes and preparations that draw to mind various regions of Colombia, from the Andean uplands to the valleys of the Magdalena River.

My husband, Diego, with the day's newspaper in hand, wakes me up with one of Bach's sonatas along with coffee's infallible presence. I ask for sounds that send me a little closer to home, and he indulges me with Alondra de la Parra's marvelous interpretation of *"Solamente una Vez."*

After rolling up the sleeves of my kimono, I look for a *chamba tiesto*—a terra-cotta earthenware plate, perfect as a griddle, and seasoned enough to suitably transfer the flavors of its own history from one arepa into the next, without overwhelming it.

Ah yes, *arepas*. Our staple corn cake, which varies widely from place to place, but is always, religiously, consumed at breakfast. So simple, yet so varied. In the mornings, I'll have one, adding only cheese or a little butter—and always with a cup of coffee. Hold the milk.

When I was fifteen, I'd have my arepa with a cold glass of Milo, Nestlé's approach to Ovaltine for the Latin American and Southeast Asian markets. Almost a milkshake. Unforgettable, so much so that I've created recipes with it throughout this book.

The sound of coffee cups clattering against their saucers declares the start of a day. For Colombians and Colombian Americans, a firmly anchored breakfast is fundamental and intrinsically woven into our ways and lifestyles. Every region concocts an astonishing array of breakfast options, from sweet boiled yuca with sesame paste and pork belly in the Sinú River valley to the well-wrapped rice *pasteles* in Santander. Culturally, breakfast is shared as a family, at times a distant reality in our busy lives.

Since breakfast is the perfect breeding ground for hangover cures, Colombians have perfected it in a variety of forms. We do the *calentao*—a philosophy more than a recipe—in which the ultimate way to use up leftovers is by chopping them into small pieces and topping it all with a crusty fried egg. We also greet the day with a much-restorative short rib broth, especially when feeling under the weather. Or we might even go for the sweet comfort of *mazamorra*, hominy with milk and *panela*. For the latter, I like to add some fruit into the mix.

Throughout my childhood, the recipes that follow helped me start the day and continue to do so today. They also comfortably come to life in any place, at any time, for anyone.

¡Buenos días!

AREPAS

Omnipresent and quintessentially Colombian, arepas are grilled, griddled, or fried cakes made of ground corn, water, and salt. Our take on the arepa is distinctly minimalist and every region has its own version, from the sweet yuca arepas of Cesar to the *anís* arepas of Magangué, from the breadfruit arepas of San Andrés to green chickpea arepas from the Tenza Valley—just to name a few. In fact, the Colombian Academy of Gastronomy published a study that reported at least seventy-two arepa variations present in the country's capital alone. But to any Colombian walking down the street, arepas are simply their native bread. Unapologetically essential to life.

In 2012, the renowned food historian from Medellín Julián Estrada wrote a lengthy article about arepas for a monthly newspaper called *Universo Centro*. In his article, titled "Tribulaciones Sobre la Arepa," he claims that "arepa means family, means mom, means homeland, means history, means strength, means perseverance." He continues, with what I can only describe as passion, "arepa is sexuality, it is ponderation, it is luck, but at the same time it is clumsiness. Paradoxically, the Antioqueños have turned this ball of dough into their most illustrious decoration by flattering themselves and strangers with a necklace of arepas." Yes, edible ground corn cake necklaces are a thing in Colombia.

A nourishment for all moments, breakfast, afternoon, and even dinner, arepas also tend to take up good space in the Colombian diaspora's freezers. I confess to bringing them to the United States, clandestinely wrapped in newspapers, just so they could keep me warm through Vermont winters in my culinary school years.

**MAKES 12 TO 15
MEDIUM-SIZE AREPAS**

1 pound dried cracked white hominy, soaked overnight, drained, and rinsed, or 2 (14.5-ounce) cans hominy, drained and rinsed (if using canned hominy, go directly to Making Arepa Dough method, and replace the cooking liquid with ½ cup water)

6 tablespoons butter, at room temperature

1 teaspoon kosher salt

½ cup warm water

6 tablespoons sunflower oil, plus more for forming the arepas

AREPAS DE MAÍZ TRILLADO

CRACKED CORN AREPAS

To make this dough you will need a manual or electric food grinder. My ultimate favorite grinder is the manual kind that attaches to the side of a table and you have to crank the handle to grind—it feels so satisfying. The process of making something from scratch, much like making homemade pasta or dumplings, is grounding, a step back from our overly high-tech lives. Every now and then, we get together with our Brooklyn friends and, between sips of wine and *aguardiente*, make a large batch of arepas that each of us can take home and freeze. A uniting feast, and breakfast is covered for at least a week.

Pressure cooker method

Rinse the soaked hominy very well. Place the dried hominy in a pressure cooker with enough water to cover by at least 4 to 5 inches. Cover with the lid and cook the hominy over high heat for 1 hour. Turn off the heat and allow the steam to escape. Once all the steam has been released, carefully remove the lid.

Large pot method

Place the soaked hominy in a large pot with enough water to cover by at least 4 to 5 inches, and over high heat bring to a boil. Reduce the heat to medium-low and simmer until the hominy is tender, about 2 hours.

Nestle a large colander into a slightly larger bowl and strain the hominy, making sure to save the excess liquid. Set aside the liquid and let the hominy cool, about 20 minutes.

Line a baking sheet with parchment paper and set aside.

Preheat the oven to 325°F.

Making the arepa dough

Place the drained hominy and ½ cup of the reserved liquid into a large food processor. Add the butter, salt, and warm water and process on low, pausing every 30 seconds or so to scrape the sides of the bowl with a rubber spatula to ensure all the hominy gets processed.

Continue processing for about 2 minutes, until you have a semi-smooth white dough. The dough will appear glossy, a bit wet, and should still have some texture from the corn. Place the dough in a well-oiled medium-size bowl. Coat your hands with oil before you start forming the arepas, as the

Continued

dough will still be a bit sticky. Form 12 balls, then flatten each one with your palms, smoothing the edges with your fingers. Each arepa should be around ½ inch thick. Place the arepas on the prepared baking sheet (see Note).

Heat a large nonstick skillet over medium-high heat. Add 2 tablespoons oil or oil spray and add as many arepas as you can without overcrowding (3 to 4). Cook undisturbed until they brown nicely, 4 to 5 minutes. Use a flat spatula to turn the arepas over and brown on the other side for another 4 to 5 minutes. Place the finished arepas on a baking sheet and keep warm in the oven. Repeat the process with the next batch, adding more oil or spray between batches, until all the arepas have been cooked.

Note: This is the perfect time to freeze the arepas if not eating immediately. Stack them in between parchment paper squares and wrap them in a reusable plastic bag. Arepas will keep well frozen for up to 2 months. To cook, simply remove from the freezer and place directly on the griddle over medium-low heat until crispy and warmed throughout, 8 to 10 minutes per side.

MAKES 6 AREPAS

2 cups pre-cooked white cornmeal or P.A.N. arepa flour

1 cup (4 ounces) grated mozzarella cheese

2 teaspoons kosher salt

6 cups water

Cooking spray

Butter

Flaky sea salt for serving

AREPAS CON QUESO

AREPAS WITH CHEESE

When you don't have time to soak, cook, and grind corn from scratch, but you still want a homemade arepa, there is the wonderful arepa flour—a pre-cooked cornmeal (*masa harina*)—used in Mexican recipes and widely available (see page 12).

In a medium metal bowl, combine the cornmeal, cheese, and kosher salt. Slowly add the water while stirring the mixture with a wooden spoon. Once the dough comes together, knead it a few times. If the dough is cracking, add 1 tablespoon of water at a time to hydrate. The final dough should be moist but not too wet. Cover with a damp cloth and let rest for 10 minutes.

After resting, the dough will feel firmer to the touch and some of the water will have been absorbed by the masa. Divide the dough into six pieces. Using your hand, shape each piece into a ¼-inch-thick round.

Heat a seasoned comal, cast-iron skillet, or griddle over medium-high heat and mist with cooking spray. Place the arepas in the pan and cook undisturbed until golden brown, 3 to 5 minutes per side.

To serve, top with butter and flaky sea salt to taste.

MAKES 6 AREPAS

For the arepas

1 cup sweet yellow
corn kernels

1 cup pre-cooked yellow
cornmeal or Masa Arepa

3 tablespoons sugar

¼ cup all-purpose flour

1 teaspoon baking powder

1 teaspoon kosher salt

1 cup *quesito* or fresh
ricotta cheese

½ cup grated Manchego
or Parmesan cheese

3 tablespoons butter, melted,
plus 2 tablespoons

¾ cup 2% milk

**For the Raw Tomato
& Avocado Salad**

2 cups ripe cherry tomatoes,
halved crosswise

2 Hass avocados, pitted,
peeled, and cubed

Juice of 1 lemon

1 tablespoon extra-virgin
olive oil

Flaky salt and freshly ground
black pepper

To serve

4 ounces *quesito* or *queso
fresco*, crumbled

½ cup cilantro leaves

AREPAS DE CHOCLO

SWEET CORN AREPAS

This arepa is a different animal, with a life and a history of its own.

The word *choclo* or *chocolo* comes from the Quechua language, which was spoken in the Incan empire for a millennium and is one of the few surviving indigenous languages in Latin America. We Colombians have adopted the word, as have many other cultures in the hemisphere. And for all, *chocolo* means the same: sweet corn.

And sweet it is indeed. So much so that nowadays, just about every street fair in New York City has a sign that reads "Mozzarepas," a registered name founded thirty-some years ago by a Colombian family in New Jersey.

Chocolo arepas are sweet and cheesy. I lean toward adding both *queso fresco* and Manchego cheese to the dough for a more interesting taste, rather than mozzarella. But I leave it up to you.... The key is to get your griddle very hot so that a nice crusty outer layer forms. In my desire to make this a full meal—breakfast for dinner, that is—I toss together a tomato and avocado salad to cut through the richness.

Grind the corn in a food processor until the kernels break apart and the mixture is smooth. Transfer the ground corn to a large bowl and add the cornmeal, sugar, flour, baking powder, salt, the *quesito*, and the Manchego cheese. Using a wooden spoon, mix the ingredients to combine. Add the 3 tablespoons butter and the milk and to stir until the mixture comes together. Do not overmix. In the beginning, your mixture will look like a very loose pancake batter. Don't fret, the cornmeal will take a few minutes to absorb the liquid and achieve a better consistency. Allow the batter to rest for 10 to 15 minutes.

Meanwhile, prepare the raw tomato and avocado *salad:* In a medium bowl, combine the tomatoes and avocados. Add the lemon juice and olive oil and toss to combine. Season with salt and pepper to taste.

Line a baking sheet with parchment paper and set aside.

Preheat a large cast-iron skillet or griddle over medium-high heat. Melt the 2 tablespoons butter until bubbles form. Measure ½ cup of the batter and pour into the pan—pancake style. You can fry the arepas 2 at a time or more, depending on the size of your skillet. Do not crowd the skillet. Cook the arepas until golden brown, 2 to 3 minutes per side. You may need to turn down the heat as you go so that the pan doesn't get too hot from batch to batch. Place the finished arepas on the baking sheet and keep warm in the oven. Repeat with the remaining batter.

To serve, plate each arepa and top with a spoonful of the tomato and avocado salad, the crumbled *quesito*, and cilantro leaves.

SERVES 4 TO 6

3 pounds English-cut
beef short ribs, cut into 2-inch
pieces by the butcher

Kosher salt

4 garlic cloves, smashed

3 scallions, trimmed and
sliced lengthwise

4 cilantro stems
(finely chop the leaves and
reserve for the *Ají Verde*)

1½ pounds medium Yukon
Gold potatoes, peeled
and quartered

3 juicy limes, halved

**For the *Ají Verde*
(Green Ají)**

1½ bunches cilantro, leaves
and stems, finely chopped
(about 2 cups)

1 green bird's eye chili or
jalapeño, finely chopped

10 tablespoons white vinegar

1 teaspoon sugar

3 tablespoons water

Kosher salt and freshly
ground black pepper

CALDO DE COSTILLA

SHORT RIB SOUP

The Paloquemao market in Bogotá opens at 5 a.m. The buzzing flower section in the rather chilly capital explodes with flowers of all varieties; carnations, orchids, roses, pompoms, agapanthus, proteas, and hydrangeas . . . it's simply a dream. Nine thousand feet above sea level, the bundles of blooming eucalyptus vie for oxygen and exude an enchanting scent. Breakfast is served around the market by women who wake up before dawn to prepare food for the early risers.

A local favorite is the *caldo de costilla*: a fork-tender short rib on the bone, with a savory, flavorful broth and potatoes. Making this soup the day before a big party or a celebration is wise—it is the ultimate hangover cure, plus cooling the broth completely will allow you to skim the fat, resulting in a clear and lighter soup. You may skip this step if you'd like and serve the soup as soon as the potatoes are cooked through.

Liberally season the short ribs with salt and place in a single layer along with the garlic, scallions, and cilantro stems in a medium-size Dutch oven, and add enough water to cover the contents 4 inches above the ribs. Bring to a boil over high heat, cover, and reduce the heat to medium-low, so that the liquid simmers slowly but ripples consistently, and simmer, about 2 hours. Add the potatoes to the broth, stir, and cook until the potatoes soften but still hold their shape, about 15 minutes.

Meanwhile make the *ají verde*: In a medium bowl, combine the cilantro, green chili, vinegar, sugar, water, and salt and pepper to taste. Stir in the reserved chopped cilantro leaves. Transfer the mixture to a serving bowl and set aside. The *ají* will become more flavorful as it sits and the flavors infuse the vinegar. The *ají* can be stored in a jar, refrigerated, for a week.

With a slotted spoon, remove the potatoes and ribs from the Dutch oven and set aside in a bowl. Strain the broth into a medium-size bowl, discarding the solids. Let stand, uncovered, until the excess fat floats to the top and solidifies, turning white.

Skim off the solid fat and strain the broth for a second time to make sure any excess fat is removed. Pour the broth back into the Dutch oven, and reheat over medium-high heat until it reaches a simmer, 5 to 7 minutes.

To serve, add 1 to 2 ribs and 2 to 3 pieces of potato to each bowl, and ladle the hot broth over the top. Serve with a side plate, so guests can use a fork and spoon to comfortably remove the meat from the rib bone and add back to the broth. Drizzle with the *ají verde*, and a good squeeze of lime. Enjoy!

SERVES 6

6 medium green bananas, peeled

1 garlic clove, peeled and smashed

1 teaspoon kosher salt, plus more to taste

6 large organic eggs

1 cup grated dried, salty cheese (*costeño, ricotta salata*, or Cotija)

3 tablespoons unsalted butter

1 tablespoon fresh lime juice

1 tablespoon extra-virgin olive oil, plus more for drizzling

3 scallions, white and green parts, thinly sliced

½ cup finely chopped cilantro leaves

Freshly ground black pepper

CAYEYE CON HUEVO Y HIERBAS

CREAMY BANANA PUREE WITH POACHED EGGS & HERBS

Magdalena is a coastal state on Colombia's Caribbean Sea surrounded by lush, endless banana plantations. This magical region is filled with so much languor and so many legends that the Nobel laureate Gabriel García Márquez chose this place as the imagined setting for his fictional Macondo in *One Hundred Years of Solitude*. Natural to this palpable magical realism is a nourishing farmer's breakfast: cooked unripe bananas pureed with butter and salty farmer cheese.

Eat slowly, mixing in the cheese with a spoon as you savor. In this version I took the liberty to add a poached egg and fresh herbs to brighten the flavors. It is most definitely a brunch favorite of mine.

Place the peeled bananas, garlic, and salt in a medium pot, cover with water, and bring to a boil over high heat. Reduce the heat to medium-low and cook until soft, 8 to 10 minutes.

Over high heat, bring a medium pot of water to a boil. Lower the heat to medium-high, and keep the water at a gentle simmer. Prepare a medium-size bowl of warm water and place near the stove. Crack 1 egg into a small strainer over a bowl and drain any watery egg white. Discard the clear liquid in the bowl. Gently slide the egg into the simmering water, and cook, for about 4 minutes, until the egg white is pulled together. Remove the egg from the water with a slotted spoon, and place into the warm water to hold while the other eggs poach. Repeat with each egg.

Remove the bananas from the heat and set aside. Discard the garlic clove and strain and reserve 1 cup of the cooking liquid. In a food processor, puree the bananas, cheese, butter, lime juice, and salt to taste. Scrape down the sides of the processor with a rubber spatula. Add ½ cup of the reserved cooking liquid and puree to soften. The mixture should be creamy but not too loose. Add some or all of the remaining ½ cup reserved liquid if it feels stiff. Transfer the mixture to a bowl and cover with foil to keep warm.

In a small saucepan, heat the oil. Add the scallions and cook, stirring, until tender and the whites begin to turn golden brown, about 2 minutes.

To serve, divide the warm *cayeye*, plus more to taste among bowls, and top with egg, 1 tablespoon sautéed scallions, and the cilantro. Finish with salt and pepper to taste.

SERVES 4 TO 6

6 cups water

3 cups 2% milk
or rice milk

5 whole scallions
(3 halved lengthwise;
2, white parts finely chopped,
for garnish)

2 cilantro stems, plus ½ cup
chopped leaves, for garnish

Kosher salt

4 ounces halloumi cheese, cut
into ½-inch pieces

6 large organic eggs

10 ounces day-old country
bread, cut into 6 chunks

CHANGUA BOGOTANA

HEARTY MILK & EGG SOUP

This soup is the quintessential cold-weather farm breakfast. Particularly in-grained in the traditions of the mountainous farmers, *changua* is to Colombians what *congee* is to the Chinese: a comforting, soothing, and savory broth.

Once, at a photoshoot in San Francisco of all places, I met a second-generation Colombian woman who came over to introduce herself because she heard I was from Bogotá. The very first thing she said after shaking my hand and proclaiming that she, too, was Colombian was: "So, how do you make *your changua*?" It took me a few seconds to process such a precise question at that moment and place. During my silence, she proceeded to share her own way: rice milk instead of cow's, because it agrees better with her.

I loved this replacement because rice milk adds a nutty taste comparable to congee. The warm cheese takes on a chewy texture and pulls with every spoon-ful as it begins to melt in the soup.

The soup is also an effective use for day-old bread, nourishing yet light. Per-fect for a cold winter morning.

Pour the water and milk into a medium pot. Add the halved scallions and cilantro stems, and season with salt to taste. Stir and bring to a gentle simmer over medium-high heat. Do not allow the milk to boil as it will break. Once steam becomes visible over the surface of the milk, lower the heat to medium-low and cook for 10 minutes. Add the cheese and stir.

Crack 1 egg into a small strainer over a bowl and drain any watery egg white. Discard the clear liquid left in the bowl and gently slide the egg into the simmering soup. Repeat with each egg. Cook for 4 minutes, until the egg whites have set and the yolks are glossed over but still jammy.

To serve, divide the bread among the soup bowls. With a spider or slotted spoon, "fish" the poached eggs and cheese pieces out of the soup and place atop the bread in the bowls. Taste the soup for salt, add a bit more if needed, and ladle the soup into the bowls, leaving the cilantro and scallion stems behind. Serve with the chopped cilantro and scallions so that each person can garnish to their liking.

SERVES 8

½ cup coconut oil, melted, plus more for oiling the pan

9 ounces yuca root, peeled and quartered lengthwise

¼ cup grapefruit juice

1 tablespoon grapefruit zest

¼ cup granulated sugar

⅔ cup loosely packed grated panela or dark brown sugar

3 large organic eggs, at room temperature

1½ cups all-purpose flour

1 teaspoon kosher salt

2 teaspoons baking powder

½ teaspoon baking soda

1 teaspoon anise seeds

For the topping
2 cups fresh coconut shavings (my trick is to put fresh coconut removed from its shell in the freezer for about ten minutes and then slice ribbons with a hand peeler)

TORTICA DE YUCA, COCO Y TORONJA

YUCA, COCONUT & GRAPEFRUIT LOAF CAKE

Alas, buying fresh yucas in America is a bit of a gamble. It's impossible to tell if it will have those unwanted bitter black veins on the inside or if it will be crisp, white, and sweet. At Colombian markets, the *marchanta* (female vendor) will crack the root open with a machete right in front of you to prove that what you are taking home is an immaculate white piece. Unfortunately, it is unlikely you'll run into a supermarket employee armed with a machete in the produce section. In this case, resorting to the frozen section of the supermarket is a great alternative, where peeled and cut yucas are easily found and ready to boil. This particular use for yuca is entirely my own.

Preheat the oven to 325°F and set an oven rack to the middle position.

Oil a 9 x 5-inch loaf pan with coconut oil and line with parchment paper. Make sure enough parchment paper hangs from the sides, so you can easily pull out the loaf from the pan.

Place the yuca quarters in a medium pot, cover with cold water, and bring to a boil over high heat. Reduce the heat to a simmer and cook until tender, 20 to 25 minutes. Drain into a colander and set aside, allowing the yuca pieces to cool slightly and release some steam.

Once cool enough to handle, remove the vein and any fibrous strands. Transfer the yuca to the bowl of a stand mixer fitted with the paddle attachment, and whisk to break up the pieces. Whisk in the grapefruit juice. Mix on low speed, adding the zest, oil, granulated sugar, and *panela*. Continue mixing until the batter is well combined. Add the eggs one by one, using a rubber spatula to scrape down the sides of the bowl after each addition.

In a separate bowl, sift together the flour, salt, baking powder, and baking soda. Add the anise seeds. Remove the bowl with the egg and yuca mixture from the stand mixer, and, using a spatula, fold in the flour mixture, a little at a time, until the batter is smooth. Pour the batter into the prepared loaf pan and smooth the top with an offset spatula or a knife. Sprinkle evenly with the fresh coconut.

Bake in the middle rack of the preheated oven until a toothpick inserted into the center of the loaf comes out clean, about 1 hour and 10 minutes. Check the cake after 45 minutes; if the coconut is browning too quickly, tent with a sheet of aluminum foil to prevent burning.

Transfer the cake to a cooling rack and allow to rest for 15 to 20 minutes before removing from the pan and slicing.

The cake will keep for up to 4 days wrapped in foil at room temperature, or for 1 month frozen.

SERVES 4 TO 6

2 (14.5-ounce) cans cooked hominy, drained and rinsed

1½ cups milk or almond milk

½ teaspoon kosher salt

2 cups blackberries, halved if large

2 tablespoons granulated sugar

Zest and juice of 1 lemon

¼ cup plain skyr or Greek yogurt, for garnish

½ cup panela, cut into small chunks, or ½ cup dark brown sugar

Edible flower petals, for garnish (optional)

MAZAMORRA CON LECHE

HOMINY WITH MILK AND BLACKBERRIES

Before dawn in the vertiginous mountains of Antioquia, the most northwest state of the country, the *arrieros*—muleteers—would begin the day with a big bowl of nourishing *mazamorra* with cold milk and chunks of sweet panela ahead of their journey. The word for corn in Spanish is *maíz*, derived from a similar sound in an indigenous language that meant "plant that sustains life."

Preparing this delicious porridge is very easy, and adding fruit to its few ingredients brightens the flavor. In this recipe I include macerated blackberries, but other fruits such as mango, plums, or pineapple will do nicely as well.

Cook the hominy, milk, and salt in a medium saucepan over medium-low heat, stirring often, until the milk is reduced and the mixture becomes thick and the hominy softens, 15 to 20 minutes. Turn off the heat, and allow the mixture to cool slightly.

Meanwhile, in a separate bowl, toss together the berries, granulated sugar, and lemon zest and juice to combine.

To serve, divide the hominy among small bowls, top with the berry mixture, and finish with a dollop of skyr or yogurt. Sprinkle with the *panela* chunks, and garnish with edible flower petals, if desired.

SERVES 6

2 tablespoons butter

1 tablespoon extra-virgin olive oil

4 large scallions, white and green parts, chopped (about 1 cup)

1 medium onion, finely chopped

6 ripe plum tomatoes, seeded and cut into ¼-inch dice (about 4 cups)

½ teaspoon kosher salt, plus more for the eggs

8 large or 10 medium organic eggs

HUEVOS PERICOS

SCRAMBLED EGGS WITH SCALLIONS AND TOMATOES

True story: Depending on the place and context, the word *perico* in Colombia might mean one of three things: coffee with a splash of milk, cocaine, or parrot. For our purposes, it's the latter, as this dish incorporates chopped green onions and red tomatoes, the colors of the bird's feathers.

Onions and tomatoes are cooked in bubbling butter and then enveloped in strands of silky, slowly scrambled eggs. Bright and colorful, *huevos pericos* are served at both Colombian and Venezuelan tables. I prefer cooking the onion and tomatoes until almost all the liquid evaporates, but many others treasure how the tomato water breaks up the eggs. Either way, the taste is heavenly.

Melt the butter in the oil in a large nonstick skillet over medium-high heat. Once the mixture begins to bubble, add the scallions and onion and stir to coat. Cook for about 2 minutes, until softened. Add the tomatoes and salt and continue cooking until the vegetables soften and the tomato water evaporates, 15 to 18 minutes.

Meanwhile, break the eggs into a medium-size bowl, add a generous pinch of salt, and whisk vigorously. Pour the beaten eggs into the tomato and scallion mixture and, with a wooden spoon, stir to combine. Cook over low heat, pushing the egg ribbons from side to side and incorporating the vegetables until the eggs are cooked to your liking, 4 to 6 minutes.

Serve immediately, accompanied by arepas or toast.

SERVES 4

3 to 4 tablespoons butter

3 white corn arepas,
torn into pieces (3 cups)

6 large organic eggs

½ teaspoon kosher salt

2 tablespoons Parmesan
cheese (optional)

MIGAS DE AREPA

Migas is the Colombian version of matzo brei. Torn, crispy arepa folded into creamy scrambled eggs. Crunchy, buttery, eggy, and so comforting. If you don't have leftover homemade arepas on hand (see page 30), not to worry—these days it's easy enough to find them at the grocery store. Look for them in the dairy section near the tortillas.

Melt the butter in a medium nonstick skillet over medium-high heat. Add the arepa pieces and cook for 3 to 5 minutes, until they are lightly browned and have absorbed most of the fat.

Meanwhile, crack the eggs into a medium-size bowl, add the salt, and whisk vigorously. Pour the eggs into the skillet with the browned arepa pieces and stir with a wooden spoon to combine. Cook over low heat, making sure you incorporate the eggs with the arepa pieces. Cook until the eggs are to your liking, 4 to 5 minutes. Garnish with the Parmesan, if using. Serve and eat while hot.

BOLLOS

The voices of teenagers walking to school right at dawn under the still cool-ish, light blue sky can be heard on the streets of the old city in Cartagena, along with the chants of the *bollo* vendors offering freshly made delights. *Los bollos, los bollos,* they chant, calling us early risers to open our balconies and step out our front doors to buy warm white corn or sweet yellow corn wrapped like tamales in fresh green corn husks, plantain leaves, or *bijao* leaves, depending on their variety and provenance.

The versatile *bollos* are served with cheese and pork belly for breakfast, and as a side starch for lunch, cut into rounds and smeared with toasted sesame paste, or split open and panfried in a bit of butter.

The state of Sucre, where my paternal family lived, is famous for its extensive *bollo* varieties: the clean white corn called *bollo limpio*, plantain, yuca, *dulce* (sweet yellow corn), *angelito* (with coconut and raisins), or *poloco* (with crispy pork bits), and many others made of rice. My father is an enthusiastic fan of this traditional breakfast food.

Colombia has a plethora of leaf-wrapped concoctions: tamales, *insulsos*, and *envueltos* (which literally means "wrapped") appear in almost all regional cuisines. Some are full meals with a piece of chicken and a whole egg inside, and others are a side or breakfast accompaniment. I love *bollos*, especially the way they are wrapped into small packages by hand using natural rope like rattan or fresh stems to firmly tie the sides and ends, coiling them together like long sausages.

Most people buy *bollos* from expert makers whose families have been selling them for generations. Making them at home is a rare and labor-intensive endeavor, so I've chosen not to include a recipe here. But no book about Colombian cuisine would be complete without at least a mention of this beloved artisanal food from my father's birthplace.

2 cups (16 ounces) cottage cheese, 4% milkfat

¾ cup masa harina or precooked white cornmeal, such as P.A.N. or Masarepa

1 tablespoon melted butter

½ teaspoon baking powder

1 teaspoon kosher salt

2 large organic eggs

2 tablespoons 2% milk

2 teaspoons orange blossom water or 2 tablespoons grated orange zest

ALMOJÁBANAS CON AGUA DE AZAHARES

ORANGE BLOSSOM WATER ALMOJÁBANAS

These pillowy cheese pastries have their origins in the Middle East. Their name comes from the word *al-muyabbana*, which in Arabic means cheese bread or cheesecake. This traditional Bogotánian pastry most likely arrived in Colombia from Syria via Spain in the sixteenth century.

Almojábanas are sold in every neighborhood bakery in brown paper bags and are even more glorious when accompanied by hot chocolate (see page 52). The dough is traditionally made with unpasteurized strained fresh cheese called *cuajada*, which is hard to find in the United States. (The FDA tends to frown upon the wonders of raw milk.) But luckily, full-fat cottage cheese does the trick.

I add the orange blossom water as a way to pay tribute to this recipe's Middle Eastern ancestry. These golden pillows with a crusty top are best served warm or right out of the oven.

Preheat the oven to 400°F.

Line two medium baking sheets with parchment paper.

In a food processor, mix the cottage cheese and cornmeal together until the cottage cheese curds break up and the cornmeal is incorporated. Add the butter, baking powder, salt, eggs, milk, and orange blossom water and process until the dough comes together. The dough may be a little sticky. Transfer the dough to a bowl, cover, and allow to rest for 10 to 20 minutes.

With damp hands, shape the dough into ping-pong–size balls, and place on the prepared baking sheets. Bake until golden brown, 25 to 30 minutes.

Serve warm.

Tip: Day-old *almojábanas* are a marvelous substitute for bread in bread pudding recipes.

SERVES 4 TO 6

24 ounces 2% milk,
or for a lighter version
combine 12 ounces water
and 12 ounces 2% milk

6 ounces bittersweet
chocolate, chopped

2 teaspoons ground cinnamon

1 teaspoon ground cloves

¼ cup light brown sugar,
or more to taste

4 ounces part-skim
mozzarella cheese, cubed
(optional, but highly
recommended)

CHOCOLATE SANTAFEREÑO

SANTAFEREÑO'S HOT CHOCOLATE WITH CHEESE

In my home, the rumbling sound of a wooden whisk frothing milk in a metal pitcher over the stove is the sound of breakfast. This isn't your usual hot cocoa. This is pure, dark, bitter, and chocolaty, with just a hint of cloves and cinnamon. It is the ultimate breakfast beverage—dare I say it surpasses even coffee?—in the high-altitude towns of the country.

Yet, what makes this Santafereño chocolate truly unique is the addition of cheese. Yes, tiny cubes of cheese are thrown in the piping-hot chocolate. They will melt in seconds, and, yes, you will use a tiny spoon to string them out of the mug and into your mouth, taking sips of the chocolate in between bites—coming one step closer to heaven in the process.

In a deep saucepan or *chocolatera*, heat the milk, chocolate, cinnamon, cloves, and sugar over medium-high heat, watching closely so the milk doesn't boil over. Mix using a whisk—or *molinillo*—so that the chocolate pieces begin to melt in the liquid. Once the chocolate is completely melted, submerge the whisk in the chocolate, and hold the handle of the whisk in between both palms, rolling the handle back and forth as if you were warming your hands or attempting to start a fire with a stick. Start slow, then work more briskly. You are looking to create a nice foamy head.

Pour the chocolaty liquid into mugs, frothing in between each pour so each person gets their share of foam. Add the cheese to each serving if desired.

Viviana Lewis

Vivi was born in Barranquilla, Colombia, a seaport city known for its festive and bustling environment. Even though she had hospitality in her blood, Vivi opted to study a more tempered career: graphic design. Her studies and line of work took her to Bogotá, where she found success as a fashion designer and opened her own Thai restaurant.

Always an entrepreneur, Vivi left Colombia for New York, where she worked for more than a decade in catering, applying her design knowledge and techniques to food. Her skill and dedication led her to work with her good friend La Nena in an endeavor that has blossomed over the past decade and a half: Palenque. This Colombian arepa hub began its life as a food truck slinging arepas all over New York City, and opened its doors as a proper restaurant a few months before the 2020 pandemic.

Vivi is Palenque's kitchen production manager, and her ethos thrives in her mastery of arepas, more so than any other type of Colombian food. Viviana knows that arepas are the basis of Colombian cooking, and she has taken advantage of New York City's global offerings to source ingredients from all over the world, turning her and partner La Nena's arepas into something healthy and nourishing.

A LA MESA

1990

pastos y
leguminosas ltda.

PABLO BURITICA

My grandmother Adela, threshold to my life in food, was a third-generation German woman raised during the early 1900s in Antioquia, Colombia's most industrious and resilient region. There, despite the vertiginous cliffs and rough terrain, people created thriving textile, coffee, and flower industries, all through hard work and discipline. She was firm and loving, and an amazing cook, baker, florist, and teacher.

Adela hosted grand family luncheons. I vividly recall the full dining table dressed in a white crochet tablecloth knit by her own hands; the black ceramic bowls nestled into woven baskets; polished silver; starched napkins; the ample, coal-black soup terrine; and those serving platters with rice, ground beef, sweet plantains, *chicharrón*, and stewed red beans.

Today, decades later, I review her handwritten recipe journal, a quarter-century-old burgundy leather notebook that my mother kept and gave to me. Lost in an index that was clear only to the author, I found a title that reads: "Menús completos para la semana"—full menus for the week.

The menus I bring to you in this chapter are inspired by the very same ones under that vague title. They are a celebration of the tradition of eating together, hosting many, and eating lots. To me, her menus and mine reflect an important Colombian ethos: the iconic recipes in our cuisine are intended to feed multiple mouths, making the communal table a place of unity and connection.

Hence, these are full menus inspired by different regions of the country. Each includes hosting tips, a playlist, and florals that set the tone for your very own Colombian feast. The country's extraordinary flowers are essential to the way I entertain. Not only are they one of our most important exports, they complete my narrative, bringing a tablescape alive. In a sense, this chapter is the heart of the book.

From the *Bogotánian ajiáco*, a three-potato soup with capers, corn, and chicken, to the creamy *mote de queso*, a cheese and *ñame* soup perfected on Colombia's Caribbean coast, this chapter includes drinks, braises, crispy empanadas, colorful salads, and decadent desserts. Some are quite traditional, and others are exclusively my own.

Regional Menus

Winds of La Heróica
Lillet & Lentils
Cauca Valley Soirée
Cachaco Cool
Medellín's Only Season
From Beirut to Sincelejo
Arusí Pacífico
Empanada Saturnalia

WINDS OF LA HERÓICA

Picture walking down steamy, colorful streets framed by balconies with cascading bougainvillea, waving a fan with your right hand and swaying your hips to the distant sounds of music perpetually playing from just about everywhere.

Oh, Cartagena de Indias, affectionately called *La Heróica* (the heroine) due to the many battles it has braved, the pirate attacks it has sustained, and the way it has stood tall with pride for 488 years. A walled colonial city with French republican and Spanish colonial architecture sprawling on the coast of the Caribbean Sea, this port town is the stage of one of the most intense love stories of all time, that of Fermina Daza and Florentino Ariza, the lovers in Gabriel García Márquez's *Love in the Time of Cholera*.

A lovely passage of that novel describes the Portal de los Dulces, a sweetshop that still exists in the heart of town. Márquez magically relates his female character's visit to this hectic place: "She went to the candy sellers sitting behind their big round jars and she bought six of each kind, pointing at the glass because she could not make herself heard over all the shouting: six angel hair, six tinned milk, six sesame seed bars, six cassava pastries, six chocolate bars, six blancmanges, six tidbits of the queen, six of this and six of that, six of everything, and she tossed them into the maid's baskets with an irresistible grace and a complete detachment from the storm clouds of flies on the syrup, from the continual hullabaloo and the vapor of rancid sweat that reverberated in the deadly heat."

Yes, at times the city's smells can be overwhelming, yet most of Cartagena's air is sensual, daring, and flavorful. If I had to pick one Colombian feast to make and eat forever, it would without a doubt be the tangy fluke crudo with pearly citrus served with fried plantains and an ice-cold glass of natural orange wine, followed by slowly braised beef in *panela*, crushed cucumber salad, and fluffy coconut rice. These flavors bring me closer to Cartagena. I grew up going to this coastal city for vacations and later in life for work, weddings, and other celebrations.

The vibe for this gathering is lush and casually delicious. It is a menu I would choose when celebrating a special event or hosting a celebratory dinner party. The *mamey* pie takes a candle or two very well. The braised meat can be cooked the day before and it is even better enjoyed the next day.

Cocktail

COCKTAIL DE PIÑA Y CIDRÓN
Pineapple Verbena Gimlet

Starters

CRUDO DE CÍTRICOS Fluke & Citrus Crudo
CINTAS DE PLÁTANO DE DON BENITO Don Benito's Crispy Plantain Ribbons

Mains

POSTA NEGRA Beef Roast Braised in Blackened Panela
ARROZ CON COCO BLANCO White Coconut Rice
PLÁTANOS EN TENTACIÓN Plantains Stewed in Coconut Milk & Orange Zest
ENSALADA DE PEPINO MACHACAO Smashed Cucumber Salad

Dessert

PIE DE MAMEY CON HELADO DE SUERO Mamey Pie with *Suero* Ice Cream

SETTING THE SCENE

This tablescape is all about color. Yes, tropical clichés come to mind, but they exist for a reason. The difference, though, is that it isn't just a mishmash of obnoxious, punchy blues, reds, and oranges. The magic relies on a well-chosen palette of complementary tones. Here, I lean toward coral reds, muted pinks, hibiscus, scarlets, and whites, which recall the peeling plaster of old walls constructed from lime and broken seashells. The table is fully dressed with small vases of orchids, leaves, ornamental pineapples, and small flowers.

Layering textiles gives character to the setting, and combining patterns is a bold way to use pieces and fabrics to make the table uniquely yours. Handsome, real, imperfect.

HOW I HOST

I always struggle with trying not to get up a million times and perpetually doing something when I host, so I've come up with a few tricks to keep myself seated and actually enjoy the rhythm of the conversation and the flow of the meal. You probably already know that making things ahead of time and preparing dishes prior to your guests' arrival is the way to go. Yes, this is true. But let's face it, this isn't always entirely realistic, and entertaining makes you responsible not only for things being tasty, but also for cleaning up spilled wine, offering seconds, and, of course, doing your best to ensure people have a good time.

So, here are a few things I do to stay put and make sure the evening is relaxing for both me and my guests:

1. Set up a self-service bar with everything your guests need to fix their own drinks. You serve the first drink, then have your guests make their own. I also suggest having them write their names on their glasses using a wax or glass pen—everyone gets one glass for the evening.
2. If you are all sitting at the table, place a few open bottles of wine for people to pour their own. If you opt for chilled, then set up a small side table near, within arm's reach, with an ice bucket to rest the wine, making sure to drape a towel over the edge of the table to catch drips.
3. At large dinners where everyone takes their own plate and finds a spot on the couch or the rug, make sure to clear the kitchen sink, putting a "guide" plate on the bottom and a set of cutlery inside a bowl of soapy water. Guests will know how to return their plates and cutlery in a way that makes it easier to clean up afterward.
4. Remember: no one else notices the mistakes you think you made. So let it go. Enjoy it all. If you do, your guests will as well.
5. NEVER APOLOGIZE. I take this from the venerable Julia Child. I love and live by this rule. You are cooking for people, inviting them into your home, and cleaning up after. So, no matter how many mistakes, or lack of this or that your food may have, own it and smile. You have done your part, and beyond.

PLAYLIST

Imagine that coveted cool summer breeze, where the temperature of your skin and the air are one and the same. Your shoulders inevitably shake a little with joy. That is Cartagena's feel and vibe. Dance to a few of these songs while pouring Pineapple Verbena Gimlets.

"Alegría" by Elia y Elizabeth
"Gopher" by Yma Sumac
"Estaba Escrito (Mambo Moruno)" by Monna Bell
"Bambu Bambu" by Carmen Miranda
"Si Si, No No" by Machito
"Guajira Ven" by Étoile de Dakar
"Insomniaque" by Brigitte
"Muñeca" by Agustín Lara
"Matildita" by La Delio Valdez
"Quimbombo" by Machito

SERVES 8

1 large ripe pineapple

2 cups cold water

16 ounces gin, very cold

8 lemon verbena
or mint leaves

Tonic water to taste

COCKTAIL DE PIÑA Y CIDRÓN

PINEAPPLE VERBENA GIMLET

The original gimlet is a British classic. This take replaces the original citrus with pineapple and an herbal touch. The key to making this drink into a batch cocktail is for the liquids to be very cold. Save shaking individual cocktails for making a cocktail or two. This cocktail can be made ahead and stored in the refrigerator the night before.

Place the pineapple straight up on a cutting board. Hold the green top with one hand and, using a serrated knife, cut the skin starting at the top, serrating straight down, following the shape of the fruit. The skin will come off in wide strips. Turn the pineapple on its axis to cut the next portion of the skin. Once the entire fruit is peeled, turn it on its side and cut off the green top. Quarter the pineapple vertically, remove the stalky core, and set aside. Cut the pineapple into chunks, place them in the blender with the water, and blend until it is completely pureed. Strain the pineapple juice through a fine mesh sieve into a pitcher and discard the fiber. You should have 32 ounces. Save the pineapple skins to make an infusion to sip as a tea. Just give them a good rinse, place in a medium pot, fill with cold water, and bring to a boil. Cover and turn off the heat. Allow to steep for 30 minutes. You can drink it either hot or cold.

Wash and dry 8 coupe or gimlet glasses and chill in the freezer.

Pour the pineapple juice and gin into a large pitcher, and stir to combine.

Right before serving, smash each lemon verbena leaf with your hands to release its oils. Rub each leaf on one side of each glass rim. Place the leaf in the glass and divide the pineapple-gin mixture over the tops. Finish with a splash of tonic to taste.

SERVES 8

½ cup fresh grapefruit juice or pomelo juice

¼ cup lime juice

2 tablespoons extra-virgin olive oil

1 red Thai chili, thinly sliced

2 teaspoons sherry vinegar

1½ pounds fluke

2 pomelos, peeled and cut into segments (use your hands to separate the meat from the white membrane) or 2 grapefruits, oranges, or tangerines

½ cup Thai basil leaves

3 tablespoons thinly sliced chives

Flaky sea salt

CRUDO DE CÍTRICOS

FLUKE AND CITRUS CRUDO

The idea of chilling your plates just for an appetizer may seem a little much, but let me tell you it does make a difference when it comes to raw fish. It's worth it: the experience changes completely because the temperature of the fish and its citrus marinade come together beautifully over a cool surface.

Get to know your seafood sources. It may be that, in your area, scallops are a better choice than fluke. Oh, how I love these tangy, herbal, and spicy flavors with thinly sliced sweet scallops! Ask the fishmonger what just came in and what their suggestion is for a perfect ceviche or crudo. They know best.

First, chill 8 rimmed salad plates for 30 minutes or longer—the plates must be very cold.

In a small bowl, combine the grapefruit juice, lime juice, oil, chili, and vinegar and whisk to combine. Slice the fluke into ¼-inch pieces and add to the citrus marinade. Allow to sit for 10 to 15 minutes. Remove the fluke from the marinade and divide equally among the 8 chilled plates, along with the pomelo segments, and drizzle with the marinade. Garnish with the basil leaves, chives, and a sprinkle of flaky sea salt.

SERVES 8

Canola oil, for frying

4 large green plantains

Kosher salt

CINTAS DE PLÁTANO DE DON BENITO

DON BENITO'S CRISPY PLANTAIN RIBBONS

Once, at a lunch at Don Benito's, the most beautiful home in the old city, when someone softly placed on the table a basket filled with a tall cloud of plantain ribbons, piled up one on top of the other. Crisp and delicate, savory and slightly sweet. As I ate them, I kept wondering how they were made. In between courses, I excused myself and found my way to the kitchen to inquire. There, I met Nayibe, a beautiful cook who had been making all of our meals during this visit. A bit hesitant at first, she wondered why I wanted to know how she makes this appetizer, which she does almost every day. She then taught me how to make the plantain ribbons by using a potato peeler to slice the plantains lengthwise right into the oil. (One of the kitchen tools I find most useful, especially here—while also oddly pretty—is a frying spider, widely used in Asian cooking.)

These plantain ribbons are delicious on their own with a bit of salt or as an accompaniment to the crudo. Either way, it is hard to stop after the first one.

Pour 2 inches of oil into a medium Dutch oven or heavy pot. Attach a deep-fry thermometer to the pot, and bring the temperature to 375°F over medium-high heat. Or, if not using a thermometer, to gauge if the oil is at the right temperature, softly drop a plantain ribbon into the pot, and if the plantain gently sizzles and gets coated in tiny oil bubbles, then the oil is ready—if the tester piece sizzles and burns, the oil is too hot. Lower the heat and wait a moment. If the tester piece lies flat in the oil without any activity or effervescence, the oil is too cold. Wait a few minutes and try again. Meanwhile, line a sheet tray or platter with paper towels.

Peel the plantains, and using a potato peeler, cut ribbons lengthwise off each plantain. Working in batches, carefully add each ribbon to the oil, no more than 6 to 8 at a time. With a spider or a slotted spoon, move the ribbons around as they fry. Pull the fried plantains out of the oil and place on the lined sheet tray. Season with salt to taste and repeat with the remaining plantain ribbons. Serve alongside the crudo.

SERVES 8 TO 10

3½ to 4 pounds boneless top blade roast

3 tablespoons kosher salt

4 tablespoons canola oil, divided

2 medium white onions, diced

6 garlic cloves, grated or minced

3 sweet chilies, seeded, deveined, and diced

3 tablespoons Worcestershire sauce

¼ cup grated panela or dark brown sugar

1 cup red wine

2 tablespoons apple cider vinegar

3½ cups beef broth

POSTA NEGRA

BEEF ROAST BRAISED IN BLACKENED PANELA

I have a particular tenderness for braising, no pun intended. Perhaps it comes from one of my first jobs while in culinary school. I assisted the brilliant author Molly Stevens in testing recipes for her award-winning book *All About Braising*. We seasoned, seared, and slow braised on Saturday afternoons, watching the snow fall atop a mountain in Vermont, all while listening to opera on Vermont Public Radio. As far away from Colombia as I had ever been, I learned how cuts of meat vary from country to country. For instance, beef ribs are cut lengthwise in Korea and across in America.

For this recipe I followed Molly's advice: a cut of beef should result in a fork-tender texture, yielding beautiful slices from its cylindrical shape. I use a top blade roast, also known as top chuck roast. The *posta* can be made the day prior and cooled before refrigerating. Serving this meat at room temperature works very well. Just warm up the sauce and drizzle it over the meat once you have plated the slices.

Season the roast with the salt. Cover and refrigerate for at least 6 hours or overnight.

Preheat the oven to 300°F.

Remove the meat from the refrigerator about 30 minutes before you begin cooking. You want the meat to come close to room temperature; pat the meat dry to ensure a dark mahogany sear.

Heat 3 tablespoons of the oil in a large Dutch oven. Add the roast and sear on all sides until a dark golden crust forms, 15 to 20 minutes.

Remove the roast using tongs and transfer to a rimmed platter.

Pour the remaining 1 tablespoon oil into the Dutch oven. Add the onions, garlic, and chilies and cook while scraping up all the flavored bits left from searing the roast at the bottom of the pan. Cook for 6 to 8 minutes, until the onions soften and begin to brown.

Add the Worcestershire sauce and *panela* and continue stirring to incorporate; the *panela* will begin to melt in a few seconds and envelop the onions nicely. Deglaze with the wine. This is where you will obtain the base and all the flavor that will go into the meat. Allow the liquid to come to a boil, 2 to 3 minutes, so that the alcohol evaporates.

Continued

Add the vinegar and broth and stir. Return the seared roast to the braising liquid in the Dutch oven, along with any juices on the platter. Cover with a sheet of parchment paper, then the lid, and carefully transfer to the oven. Set the timer for 1 hour and 30 minutes.

Check the roast, carefully removing the lid and the paper—be careful, the steam will be very hot—and turn the roast over. Make sure there is still plenty of braising liquid. Cover again and return to the oven for another 1 hour and 30 minutes. Remove the pan from the oven, uncover, and lift the *posta* from the braising liquid. Transfer to a platter and tent with foil.

Bring the braising liquid—now your sauce—back to a boil and let cook for 5 to 6 minutes, so that the sauce thickens and the flavors concentrate. Taste for salt.

Cut the *posta* with a sharp knife into thin slices. The meat will tend to fall apart, so don't worry about getting chunky pieces—this means it is so, *so* tender and tasty.

Arrange on a platter with enough of a rim to hold a drizzle of the sauce. Serve with extra sauce on the side.

SERVES 8

2 medium coconuts with their water or 1 (14.5-ounce) can coconut milk diluted with water to make 6 cups

3 cups long-grain white rice

1½ teaspoons salt

ARROZ DE COCO BLANCO

WHITE COCONUT RICE

It's 5 a.m. Deep in the dark and mysterious alleys of Bazurto, the main market of the city, Afro-Colombian women in long ruffled skirts and turbans shred freshly opened coconuts into aluminum vats with homemade metal graters that sit precariously between their thighs, close to the floor. While some women turn the nutty fruit into shards, others take the fluffy white pieces and squeeze them between their palms to extract the richest, most concentrated coconut milk. Getting the most out of the coconut's meat is paramount. The dry fiber that's left will later be turned into *cocadas*—sweetened coconut candy. Nothing goes to waste.

There are two versions of *arroz con coco*: White Coconut Rice and Caramelized Coconut Rice (recipe follows on page 77). They both use milk from fresh coconuts, but the caramelized version includes a reduction with the first milk of the coconut and panela called *titoté*. I've included both because I simply couldn't choose one version over the other!

1. **Open a fresh coconut:** Very carefully, insert the tip of a metal skewer or paring knife into one of the three coconut "eyes" (only one of them will be soft enough to pierce through) and shake the coconut water into a glass. You can drink it right away or reserve it in the fridge for later. Repeat with the remaining coconut.

Hold the empty coconut on your hand, and you'll see a "vein" that runs around the shell. This is the breaking point of the coconut. Firmly hold the coconut on your hand, and using a hammer or a metal meat mallet, firmly tap along the vein as you turn it on your hand. A couple rounds of firm blows will crack open the coconut.

2. **Extract the flesh from the coconut:** Using the hammer, break the opened coconut into smaller pieces, making it easier and safer to handle. Carefully insert the tip of the paring knife between the coconut's inner shell and the coconut meat and separate them. What you are going for is the white meat of the coconut with its brown lining. This brown lining is what contains the coconut oil, and you want that.

3. **Make fresh coconut milk:** Using a box grater, grate the coconut meat through the large holes, or you can use a food processor with the grater attachment. At this point, the grated coconut can be stored in a zip-top plastic bag in the freezer for up to three months.

Continued

A LA MESA

Place the grated coconut in a high-speed blender with just enough warm water to barely cover the coconut and blend for 2 to 3 minutes, until you have milk.

Place a cheesecloth or a fine-mesh sieve over a medium bowl and pour the milk through, making sure you squeeze the pulp and extract all the milk.

Return the pulp to the blender, add more water, and repeat the process. Strain to extract as much milk as possible. You will need a total of 6 cups of liquid to cook the rice. Reserve.

Make the rice: Wash the rice under cold water and drain. Repeat until the water runs clear. Set aside. Place the fresh coconut milk or diluted canned coconut milk in a large heavy-bottom pan. Bring to a simmer over medium-high heat, add the rice, and season with salt. Stir the rice occasionally as it simmers so that it doesn't stick to the bottom, and cook for 10 to 12 minutes. When almost all the coconut milk is absorbed, cover the rice and lower the heat to low. Cook the rice, undisturbed, until it puffs up and it is cooked through, about 15 minutes. Fluff with a wooden spoon and serve.

SERVES 8

2 medium coconuts with their water or 16 ounces frozen grated coconut, thawed (to open a fresh coconut, see page 75)

3 tablespoons panela or dark brown sugar

3 cups long-grain white rice

1 tablespoon kosher salt

1 cup raisins

ARROZ CON COCO Y PASAS

CARAMELIZED COCONUT RICE WITH RAISINS

What makes this rice so delightful is the *titoté:* a caramel made with coconut milk and panela, which envelops the grains of rice and gives it a sweet nutty flavor. The infallible combination of the sweet and salty, and the fluffy.

Extract the coconut's first and second milk: In a high-speed blender, combine the fresh or frozen grated coconut with just enough warm water to barely cover the coconut, and blend for 2 to 3 minutes, until you have milk.

Place a cheesecloth or a fine-mesh sieve over a medium bowl and pour the mixture into the cheesecloth. Squeeze the pulp and extract all the milk, reserving the pulp. This milk is called "first milk." It is thick and fatty, and you will need 1¼ cups to make the *titoté.* Set aside this "first milk."

Return the leftover pulp to the blender, cover with 6 cups warm water, and blend. Repeat the process to extract the "second milk." You will need a total of 6 cups liquid. This "second milk" is very watery and used to cook the rice. Set aside this "second milk."

Wash the rice under cold water and drain. Repeat until the water runs clear. Set aside.

Make the *titoté*: In a large heavy-bottom pot over high heat, bring the "first milk" to a boil. Lower the heat to medium-high and simmer for 20 minutes, scraping the sides of the pot with a wooden spoon every 5 minutes. The coconut fat will begin to adhere to the sides of the pot and there will be bigger, thicker bubbles. Add the *panela* and stir well with a wooden spoon. Simmer for 6 to 7 minutes, stirring often to allow for an even browning of the *panela* with the coconut fat: the fat separates and brown bits of caramelized *panela* and coconut will form. Lower the heat to medium and keep cooking the browned bits for 3 to 4 minutes, until they become very brown. Be very careful: this browning is done to give the rice its color and caramelized coconut-y flavor, but these bits of *panela*/coconut can easily burn.

Make the rice: Add the rice and salt to the *titoté* and stir to coat the rice. Add the "second milk" and raisins and stir well, making sure you scrape the bottom of the pot.

Raise the heat to high and bring to a boil. Boil for 5 to 6 minutes without stirring, then lower the heat to low and cover with the lid.

Cook covered for 15 to 18 minutes. Open the lid and "turn" the rice over from the bottom of the pot to the top by scraping it with a large kitchen spoon. This is done for even cooking. Taste for doneness and cook a bit longer it needed.

SERVES 8

1 cup (8 ounces) canned
coconut milk

1 cup water

¼ cup grated panela
or dark brown sugar

½ teaspoon ground cloves

2 cinnamon sticks

Zest and juice of
1 large orange

4 ripe large plantains (skin
deep yellow with dark spots)

PLÁTANOS EN TENTACIÓN

PLANTAINS STEWED IN COCONUT MILK & ORANGE JUICE

It would be sacrilegious not to include a recipe for this classic and beloved dish in this book. One of the many versions of this recipe includes the locally made soft drink Kola Román as an ingredient. The Román family came up with the bright red syrup to make this popular Colombian drink back in 1865. In addition to the soft drink, the family gave the country another national treasure: Mrs. Teresita Román de Zurek, the family's heiress, who was also a resplendent writer, host, and author of *Cartagena de Indias en la Olla*, a wonderful 1960s cookbook about the food of Cartagena. Since then, the book has had more than thirty-six editions. (The latest edition styled by yours truly.) As a student, I consulted Román de Zurek's cookbook many times while learning about iconic dishes. This recipe is an adaptation from her book.

In a large skillet over high heat, stir together the coconut milk, water, *panela*, cloves, cinnamon sticks, and orange juice. Bring to a simmer and cook until the liquid starts to thicken and is reduced by half, about 10 minutes. Peel the plantains and add to the skillet. Cover the skillet and lower the heat to medium-low. Cook, basting from time to time, until the plantains are soft when pierced with a knife but still hold their shape, about 18 minutes.

To serve, cut the plantains into 3 to 4 pieces each, drizzle with the sauce, and garnish with the orange zest.

SERVES 8

5 to 6 Persian cucumbers,
cut into spears

2 garlic cloves, grated
or finely chopped

3 tablespoons white vinegar

Juice of 2 large limes
(about ½ cup)

2 teaspoons kosher salt

3 tablespoons extra-virgin
olive oil

ENSALADA DE PEPINO MACHACAO

SMASHED CUCUMBER SALAD

I chose this salad to lighten the menu and balance out the rich flavors and creamy textures with sharp and crisp tones. I prefer using Persian or Kirby cucumbers, which are full of flavor, but you can also use English cucumbers. Simply slice the cucumber in half crosswise and remove the seeds with a melon baller or a teaspoon—there is too much water in the seeds. Smashing the cucumber opens the membranes to welcome the dressing deep into the flesh, making every bite as refreshing and flavorful as it can be.

I also love serving this cucumber salad over rice with some white anchovies or tuna packed in olive oil as a very easy lunch.

Using a heavy knife, place the blade flat on a cucumber spear, and, carefully pressing the heel of your hand down onto the blade, smash the cucumbers. Repeat with the remaining spears, and transfer the smashed cucumbers to a bowl. Add the garlic, vinegar, lime juice, salt, and olive oil and stir to incorporate. Refrigerate for at least 30 minutes before serving.

Dessert

COLOMBIANA

SERVES 8 TO 12

For the crust

2½ cups all-purpose flour

2 teaspoons powdered sugar

1 teaspoon kosher salt

1½ sticks unsalted butter, chilled and diced

2 tablespoons apple cider vinegar, chilled

½ cup ice water

3 tablespoons whole milk, for brushing

For the filling

3 pounds very ripe fresh *mamey* (2 to 3 each) or 3 pounds very ripe persimmons, peeled and sliced

¼ cup grated panela or light brown sugar

1 teaspoon ground cardamom

¼ teaspoon ground allspice

½ teaspoon kosher salt

PIE DE MAMEY CON HELADO DE SUERO

MAMEY PIE WITH SUERO ICE CREAM

In Cartagena and throughout Colombia, the Benedetti name is synonymous with power and politics. Yet one special member of this family, Rosita, made the Benedettis a household name for something else: her pies. Mamey (see page 17) and coconut are at the top of my list. This recipe is my own version.

Make the crust: Pulse the flour, powdered sugar, salt, and butter in the bowl of a food processor until the mixture is the consistency of sand and comes together when pressed between the fingers. Add the apple cider vinegar and pulse a few more times. Add ¼ cup of the ice water and pulse to bring the dough together. If it feels too dry, add more water 1 tablespoon at a time, pulsing after each addition, until the dough feels moist. Remove the dough from the food processor and divide into 2 pieces, forming each piece into a disc. Wrap in plastic wrap and refrigerate for at least 30 minutes.

Meanwhile, make the filling: Cut each *mamey* in half lengthwise. Remove the brown shiny seed and, with a spoon, scoop out the creamy flesh and place in a medium bowl. In a small bowl, combine the *panela*, cardamom, allspice, and salt. Sprinkle over the *mamey* and stir to coat. If using the persimmons, simply toss the pieces with the *panela*, cardamom, allspice, and salt.

Preheat the oven to 400°F.

Remove one disc of dough from the refrigerator. On a lightly floured surface, roll the disc out to a 12-inch circle and place it in a 10½ x 2-inch pie pan. Add the *mamey* filling, mounding it in the center and leaving the edges clean. Transfer the pie to the freezer while you make the top crust.

Dust your work surface with more flour and roll out the second piece of dough to a 12-inch circle. Press the cutter in a linear pattern (leaving a 1½-inch edge uncut), saving the cutouts on the side. Remove the pie from the freezer and, with the help of the rolling pin, carefully drape the top over the *mamey* filling and close the edges together. Trim the excess dough and tuck underneath the bottom layer. Brush with the milk and place the cutouts on the edges of the pie, brushing them with the milk as well.

Return the pie to the freezer for 15 to 30 minutes.

Place the pie on a baking sheet straight from the freezer. Bake in the preheated oven for 15 minutes. Lower the oven heat to 350°F and continue to bake until the pie is an even golden brown, 35 to 40 minutes. Transfer the pie to a cooling rack. Serve cool or warm with Suero Ice Cream (recipe follows) or vanilla ice cream.

MAKES 1 QUART

3¾ cups *labneh*
(if you don't have *labneh*,
use 3¾ cups plain 2% Greek
yogurt with 3 tablespoons
lime juice stirred in)

¼ cup fruity extra-virgin
olive oil

1 pinch of sea salt

HELADO DE SUERO

SUERO ICE CREAM

This ice cream is made with *labneh* in place of traditional *suero* (see page 15), drizzled with very fruity olive oil—the one you would only use in salads or as a garnish. I love small makers such as Brightland and De Carlo Contrada San Martino.

Stir together the *labneh* and sea salt in a medium bowl. Chill for at least 30 minutes. Transfer the mixture to an ice cream maker, and follow the manufacturer's instructions. Once the frozen yogurt is creamy and set, drizzle in the olive oil and fold in partially. Cover and freeze until ready to serve.

Alternatively, place the mixture in the freezer for about 40 minutes, until it begins to set. Remove the mixture from the freezer and stir vigorously a few times with a spatula or a wooden spoon and return to the freezer for another 30 minutes. The idea here is to incorporate some air into the mixture as it freezes. Repeat 3 to 4 times and drizzle with the olive oil before serving. The ice cream will not be as creamy as if you used an ice cream machine, but the flavor will be just as good.

LILLET & LENTILS

A late afternoon lunch for eight begins with a fervent shake of bitter orange juice, Lillet, and flamenco, adding just the punch needed to begin this celebration. Lillet is an aromatized wine from Podensac, France, that I fell in love with the moment I tasted it and has become the signature aperitif in our home.

Anchoring the menu with smoky lentils made earlier in the day means only a few things are left to be prepared before guests arrive—there is no need to be a flustered host.

We ease in with a playlist to the tunes of Bebo & Cigala and others, as we reminisce about Almodóvar movies. The Spanish touch in our Colombian cuisine is undeniable, not only in its flavors, but also in its aesthetic and traditions.

Cockail

NARANJA AGRIA Y LILLET FIZZ
Bitter Orange & Lillet Fizz

Mains

ENSALADA DE AGUACATE Y CILANTRO
Cilantro & Avocado Salad
LENTEJAS AHUMADAS CON CHORIZO
Smoky Lentils with Chorizo
ARROZ BLANCO CON PLATANITOS DULCES
Rice with Crispy Sweet Plantains

Dessert

POSTRE DE COCO DE LA TIA LILITA
Tia Lilita's Coconut Custard

SETTING THE SCENE

Ideally the table would be set with a combination of tropical and lush wildflowers. Loosely place tiny roses, yellow ginger flowers, and wild black-eyed Susans into small glasses and pitchers.

Everyone should have a statement soup terrine—a vessel that becomes the focal point of the table and holds the food warm. Flea markets and antiques stores often have them, but beware, you may be tempted to start collecting them.

I love the look of an embroidered, handmade tablecloth layered on top of a solid burlap or a neutral linen. Classic yet bold. I use simple short glasses to serve the cocktail, wine, or water. It's an elegant yet unfussy way to serve drinks of everyone's choice without having too many elements on the table.

HOW I HOST

It is so lovely to sit at a table with an ironed cloth napkin on your place setting. Taking the time to iron each piece of fabric is a kind of ritual for me; I meditate to it. But I know we don't always have time for this. This is why I recommend owning a set of large linen dinner napkins. These look and feel gorgeous whether they are pressed or not. In the end it is all about the harmonious way you and your guests interact with the objects at the table.

And speaking of guests . . . flowers and wine are always an option when you're attending a dinner party, but let's avoid being predictable. On my trips around the world I always look for objects that embody the character and soul of wherever I've been—tiny seashell spoons, a bag of special salt, a jar of homemade jam from a market upstate, a little china doll bought at the night market in Shanghai—these inexpensive bits and bobs carry with them stories from these faraway places. Bringing your host something that you've selected is personal, and shows that you appreciate them.

Another host gift that I favor is a crusty baguette, a funky cheese, and a yummy jam or fruit for your generous friends to have for breakfast the next day—do say so when handing over the bag. Nothing better than waking up to a delicious, "already made" breakfast after a night of entertaining.

PLAYLIST

Play these songs when preparing and serving the Lillet & Lentils menu. We lunch and kiss the afternoon goodbye, easing into an early night festivity.

"Lágrimas Negras" by Diego el Cigala, Bebo Valdés
"Move Along" by Salt Cathedral
"Cachita" by Orquesta Aragón
"South American Way" by Carmen Miranda
"Pepito" by Las Taradas
"Mack the Knife" by Dave Van Ronk
"Soledad y el Mar" by Natalia Lafourcade
"Total" by Olga Guillot
"Stanislas" by Brigitte Bardot
"My Destiny" by Yma Sumac
"Tu Rumba" by iLe

SALAMANCA

Aji
SOBREMESA

Pieris Pinos
Colombia

SERVES 8 SMALL GLASSES

8 ounces Lillet

Juice of 5 bitter oranges
(about 24 ounces)

4 ounces sweet vermouth

Lots of ice

Orange slices,
for garnish

Club soda to taste

NARANJA AGRIA Y LILLET FIZZ

BITTER ORANGE & LILLET FIZZ

Bitter oranges are such a special citrus variety. It is fascinating how nature can pack so many flavors into one single fruit. Imagine how the complexity of this citrus—sweet, sour, bitter—comes together with the notes of my beloved Lillet, creating a refreshingly delicious aperitivo.

If bitter oranges are not in season (usually January and February are the peak for citrus in the United States), I resort to a great bottled bitter orange juice called sour orange and sold in the Latin American sections of many grocery stores. As an alternative, a dash or two of Angostura bitters added to freshly squeezed orange juice will do the trick.

Combine the Lillet, bitter orange juice, and vermouth in a medium pitcher. Pour into ice-filled glasses. Top with a splash of club soda and garnish with an orange slice.

SERVES 8

4 ripe Hass avocados, pitted, peeled, and sliced

Juice of 2 large limes (about ½ cup)

¼ cup extra-virgin olive oil

Sea salt and freshly ground pepper

2 cups cilantro leaves, washed and spun dry

ENSALADA DE AGUACATE Y CILANTRO

CILANTRO & AVOCADO SALAD

This is a creamy, citrusy, and beautiful salad that complements and balances the rich lentils. If you return from the market and find that your avocados are not quite ripe, place them in newspaper or a paper bag overnight and you will have soft avocados in the morning.

Arrange the avocado slices on a handsome platter. Drizzle with the lime juice and olive oil and gently toss. Season with salt and pepper to taste. Garnish with the cilantro and serve.

LENTEJAS AHUMADAS CON CHORIZO

SMOKY LENTILS WITH CHORIZO

SERVES 6 TO 8

2 cups dried green lentils

3 very ripe medium plum tomatoes, cut in half lengthwise

1 medium yellow onion, peeled and quartered

1 medium head garlic, skin on, sliced in half crosswise, or 4 garlic cloves, peeled

Kosher salt and freshly ground pepper

3 tablespoons extra-virgin olive oil, plus more as needed

2 medium carrots, peeled and cut into ¼-inch dice

1 small leek, white and pale green parts only, rinsed well and diced

1½ tablespoons smoked paprika

1 large fresh bay leaf

¼ cup sherry

6 cups organic chicken stock

1 tablespoon sherry vinegar or red wine vinegar

1¼ pounds Colombian or Spanish pre-cooked chorizo, diced

Lentils tend to be either beloved or despised... and my husband falls into the latter camp. So I wait patiently for him to leave for a work trip, and then make a big pot of lentils and invite everyone over. As for choosing a lentil variety for soups, I go with green or brown lentils; French du Puy or beluga are amazing for salads and sides because they hold their shape and don't get mushy.

Rinse the lentils and cover with cold water in a medium bowl. Soak for at least 3 hours. (With brown lentils, rinse and soak for 20 minutes.)

Heat a *comal*, medium-size griddle, or cast-iron pan over high heat until it is piping hot. (You can also use a *tiesto* if you have one.) Place the tomatoes, onion, and garlic, cut side down, onto the *comal* and char, turning occasionally with kitchen tongs so that all sides of the vegetables get nice and charred, 15 to 18 minutes. Don't be afraid to get the vegetables dark—this is what will give dimension and a smoky taste to your lentils.

Turn off the heat and allow the vegetables to sit on the *comal* for 5 minutes. Peel off the skins of the tomatoes with the tongs. Discard the skins.

Squeeze the garlic cloves into the bowl of a food processor or blender and discard the papery skins. Add the onion and peeled tomatoes. Using a rubber spatula, scrape all the charred bits and goodness off the pan into the processor and puree until smooth. Season with 1 teaspoon salt and ½ teaspoon black pepper, and set aside. I call this a charred veggie puree.

In a large Dutch oven or other heavy-bottom pan, heat the olive oil over medium-high heat and add the carrots, leek, smoked paprika, and bay leaf. Stir to coat in the oil. Cook until the leek begins to soften, 3 to 4 minutes. Add the drained lentils and sherry and stir to combine. Allow the sherry to bubble up and evaporate the alcohol away, 1 to 2 minutes.

Pour in the charred veggie puree and give it another stir. Cook for a few minutes, until everything begins to bubble—this way you are building flavor as you add the ingredients. Add the chicken stock, season with salt and pepper to taste, and bring to a boil. With a wooden spoon, stir the lentils, then lower the heat to medium-low. Cook for 30 to 35 minutes, making sure you stir and scrape the bottom of the pan every 10 minutes with a wooden spatula, until the lentils are tender but still hold their shape. Add the sherry vinegar, stir, and taste, adjusting the seasoning as needed.

Continued

As you are working on the lentils, heat a large skillet over medium heat. Add the chorizo. You may or may not need oil for the chorizo to brown; it should begin to render its own fat as it heats up. If it is looking too dry, drizzle in 1 teaspoon olive oil. Cook for 5 to 6 minutes, until nicely browned. I like cooking the chorizo separately so that it is still juicy and not overcooked—not to mention the fact that you can keep the lentils meatless for a mixed crowd. Drain the fat and add the chorizo to the lentils, or keep separate to serve on the side.

Ladle the lentils into bowls, and serve with White Rice with Sweet Plantains (recipe follows) and Cilantro & Avocado Salad (page 94).

ARROZ BLANCO CON PLATANITOS DULCES

WHITE RICE WITH SWEET PLANTAINS

SERVES 8

2½ cups long-grain
white rice

2 tablespoons kosher salt

2 cups vegetable or
canola oil

3 very ripe medium plantains
(skin almost black), peeled
and cut into ¼-inch cubes

2 tablespoons sugar

Cooking perfect rice is an art form. Every cook has their preferred formula and method. As a food stylist working on photography sets, I learned to make rice the easiest way possible: boiled in abundant salted water and drained. The result is loose grains of perfectly flavored rice. Some may frown upon this method, but I tell you, it never fails!

Wash the rice under cold water and drain; repeat until the water runs clear. Set aside.

Bring a large pot of water with the salt to a boil. Add the rice and stir a few times to prevent the grains from sticking to the bottom. Cover and cook, undisturbed, for 15 to 18 minutes, until the rice is puffed and soft but not mushy. Drain the rice, transfer back to the pot, and cover to keep warm.

In the meantime, heat the oil in a medium saucepan to 350°F, checking the temperature with a deep-fry thermometer. You can also test if the oil is at the right temperature without a thermometer by adding one cube of the plantain into the heated oil; if it sizzles surrounded by tiny bubbles without burning too fast, then it is ready. Scatter the sugar on a plate or in a shallow pie pan and set aside. Add the plantain cubes to the oil in batches, constantly moving them around in the oil using a slotted spoon or spider, and fry until golden brown, about 3 minutes. Scoop the plantain cubes from the oil and roll in the sugar—churro style—to coat. Reserve on the side on a separate platter while you make the other batches.

Serve the rice on a platter topped with the fried plantains.

SERVES 8

12 ounces fresh
coconut meat, grated
(1 medium fresh coconut
or 3 cups frozen grated
coconut, thawed;
see how to get meat from
a whole coconut,
page 75

½ cup sugar

1 tablespoon lemon juice

2 cups heavy cream

1 (14-ounce) can sweetened
condensed milk

3 large organic eggs,
yolks and whites separated

½ cup milk

¼ teaspoon cream of tartar

POSTRE DE COCO DE LA TIA LILITA

TIA LILITA'S COCONUT CUSTARD

This flan is best made the day before so it can be completely chilled when it comes time to slice it. I learned to make it using a double boiler flan pot, but my recipe uses the oven method—no need to buy one more piece of cookware!

The caramel and batter can be divided into 8 custard cups for a more refined presentation, if you'd like.

Preheat the oven to 350°F.

Add the sugar to a medium skillet and cook over medium heat, without stirring, until it melts and starts to take on an amber color. Swirl the pan so that the sugar is incorporated and caramelizes evenly and cook for about 5 minutes. Carefully add the lemon juice (this may cause the hot caramel to splatter), stir, then pour the caramel into a 9-inch cake pan. Swirl the pan around so that the caramel thinly coats the bottom.

In a large bowl, combine the grated coconut, heavy cream, condensed milk, egg yolks, and milk, using a hand mixer to blend.

In another large bowl, whisk the egg whites and cream of tartar with an electric mixer starting on low speed, moving gradually to high speed, until stiff peaks form, 5 to 6 minutes. With a rubber spatula, gently fold the egg whites into the milk and coconut mixture until combined.

Pour the mixture into the caramel-coated cake pan.

Meanwhile, bring a medium saucepan of water to a boil.

Place the cake pan in a large roasting pan and transfer to the oven. With the door open, carefully pour enough boiling water into the roasting pan to reach halfway up the cake pan's side. Bake until the custard no longer shakes and looks firm, about 1 hour and 20 minutes. Tent with foil after 30 minutes to avoid the top browning too quickly. Lift the cake pan from the hot water and let it cool completely. Place in the fridge overnight or for a minimum of 6 hours to reach optimal texture. Invert the custard onto a large rimmed platter. Cut into wedges and serve. This dessert keeps covered in the refrigerator for up to 3 days.

CAUCA VALLEY SOIRÉE

Vast sugarcane plantations sway in the warm breeze of the lush Cauca River valley, home to the city of Cali—the world's capital of salsa dancing. This is a region where music resonates in people's hips and spicy ají flavors every party. Zest and passion are the pillars of this region.

This is a soiree inspired by the dappled light of the imposing ceiba trees, the rich boozy taste of crushed sugarcane distilled into *aguardiente*, and Johanna Ortiz's gowns endlessly flowing throughout Cali's outdoor dance floors.

The menu may look a bit laborious at first glance. But here's the trick: make the empanadas and dessert in advance. While you're at it, remember to always keep an extra batch of empanadas in the freezer ready to pop in the oven or fry up when needed.

And don't worry about the main dish, the *sancocho* "prepares itself, over low heat without any special attention," a direct quote from *El Gran Libro de la Cocina Colombiana*, by Carlos Ordóñez Caicedo (1987). You simply add the roots and meats to the pot in the right order and the rest sorts itself out.

Cocktail

LULADA "ENVENENADA"
Chunky Lulo with Aguardiente

Starters

EMPANADITAS DE PIPIÁN Potato & Peanut Empanadas
AJÍ DE MANÍ Spicy Peanut Sauce
PANDEBONO Rice Bread Puffs

Main

SANCOCHO Beef, Pork & Chicken Stew

Dessert

ESPONJADO DE LIMÓN
Lime Mousse

SETTING THE SCENE

Think large green leaves, small potted plants, a weighty linen striped tablecloth, mix-and-match earthen-ware. You can sprinkle in terra-cotta and white ceramics, bamboo flatware, and vintage napkins—layer and combine materials and textures to give the table a casual, airy feel.

Passing the appetizers in rustic platters and leaf-lined trays is a chic way for everyone to mingle, eat, and sip their *luladas* or chilled wine while things loosen up and everyone relaxes.

HOW I HOST

Sancocho feeds many. It's easier to serve this dish as a buffet, making it a whole experience. I sort of despise the word *buffet*. It makes me think of corporate banquet rooms with those shiny polyester table-cloths or the ever-dreadful lines at weddings. Set a splendid side table with the broth, roots and meats on platters, generous avocado slices lined on a board, and rice in a terrine to keep warm. At times, when there are more than eight people over, I'll serve two platters of each component on each side of the table, just so that the line moves quicker.

Usually, one or two guests will offer to help the moment they arrive. I'll keep my eyes open for them, and when it's time to serve, I'll ask them to do so lovingly. This way, everyone gets food quickly, and feels involved, and we can all enjoy a bowl of broth while it's actually still warm.

Normally, I set the table with a few bowls of ají in the center, as well as some flaky sea salt for everyone to sprinkle on as they please. A couple buckets of ice for a few bottles of crisp Verdejo are set on a side table. Lunch is served.

PLAYLIST

Play this when preparing and serving the Cauca Valley Soiree menu.

"Humo" by La Sonora Matancera
"I like It Like That" by Pete Rodriguez
"Con Una Sola Miradita" by Celia Cruz
"I'll Play the Fool" by Claude Fontaine
"Tú Me Acostumbraste" by Carlotta Cosials
"Marilu" by George Guzman
"Maracaibo Oriental" by Benny Moré
"That's How Rumors Start" by Joey Pastrana and His Orchestra
"Salsa Y Dulzura" by Ray Barretto
"Enamorate Bailando" by Septeto Acarey
"Guaranco Perfecta" by La Perfecta

SERVES 8

¼ cup finely grated panela or light brown sugar

½ cup boiling water

3 pounds whole frozen *lulos*, cut in half with the meat scooped out, or 2 pounds frozen *lulo* pulp (also known as *naranjilla*), or 3 pounds green mango, peeled, seeded, and cut into chunks

3 dashes orange bitters or Angostura bitters

1 tablespoon grated orange or tangerine zest

8 ounces chilled aguardiente or vodka

10 cups medium ice cubes

Tangerine leaves or basil leaves, for garnish (optional)

LULADA "ENVENENADA"

CHUNKY LULO WITH AGUARDIENTE

Street food in Cali is known for its mostly refreshing slushies: ice cold corn and pineapple *champús* (page 221), frappés with fruit and sweetened condensed milk or *cholados*, and the *lulada*—a chunky sour and slightly sweet drink that I "poison" with aguardiente, a distilled sugarcane-and-anise liqueur that flavors all parties, festivals, weddings, and even christenings across the country. Orange bitters are my secret addition to these spiked *luladas*. I recommend serving them in highball glasses with lots of ice and a long spoon to reach those *lulo* chunks.

In a glass measuring cup, dissolve the panela in the boiling water.

Place the *lulo* in a large pitcher. Using a wooden spoon, crush the pulp into chunks. If you are using whole fruit, you will want to break it into small pieces, and if you are using the frozen pulp, the idea is to break it up as well. Add the dissolved *panela*, bitters, zest, *aguardiente,* and ice. Stir a few more times to incorporate ice into the sweetened fruit. Pour in 6 cups cold water, stir, and divide into 8 highball glasses with a long spoon. Garnish with a tangerine leaf.

MAKES ABOUT 65 EMPANADAS

2 cups warm water,
plus more as needed

1 tablespoon vegetable oil

1 tablespoon grated panela
or brown sugar

2 cups yellow *masa harina*
(see page 12 for brands)

¼ cup yuca flour
or cornstarch

2 teaspoons kosher salt

1 quart Pipián Filling
(recipe follows)

Canola oil, for frying

1 egg, beaten, for baking

Equipment
Tortilla press lined with
plastic wrap or small heavy
skillet such as a cast-iron pan

Two baking sheets lined with
parchment paper

Ají de Maní (recipe follows),
for serving

3 to 4 limes, cut into small
wedges, for serving

EMPANADITAS DE PIPIÁN

MINI POTATO & PEANUT EMPANADAS

Tiny, savory, sublime empanadas made with a red filling of potatoes, peanuts, and *achiote* can either be baked or fried. Naturally, fried is the traditional way and the most delicious, but if you, like me, sometimes don't have it in you to deep-fry, the oven method works just fine. Serve with Ají de Maní (peanut sauce, recipe follows) on the side.

Empanada dough is a delicate beast—the moisture in the air and, if you are superstitious, the mood of the cook, will affect how much water you'll actually need for the dough to be just right.

In a glass measuring cup, stir together the water, oil, and *panela* until the *panela* is dissolved. In a large bowl, mix together the *masa harina*, yuca flour, and salt. Pour the *panela* mixture in a steady stream into the dry ingredients until it comes together; it should look like moist sand. Knead a few times to incorporate and form a dough. Test the consistency between your fingers: the dough should be moist but neither too wet nor too dry. If needed, add more water, one tablespoon at a time, until the texture is pliable and not dry. Cover the dough with a damp kitchen towel and use right away.

Place 1 heaping tablespoon (1½ ounces) of the dough in between the two pieces of plastic wrap in the center of the tortilla press. The key is to press slightly more gently than you would if making tortillas. Each disc should be 3½ inches in diameter: if it is bigger it will be too thin and will rip. If using a heavy skillet, also place a heaping tablespoon of dough between plastic wrap and press down with the skillet.

Fill each masa disc with 1 tablespoon of the *pipián* filling, wet the edge of the dough with water, and fold over to seal in a half-moon shape. You can mend any cracks on the dough by wetting your finger and rubbing a bit of water over it.

Transfer the empanada to the prepared baking sheet. Repeat with the remaining dough. When you have made all the empanadas, transfer them to the freezer for at least 20 to 30 minutes to firm up before frying or baking.

To Fry
Pour 2 inches of canola oil into a medium Dutch oven or heavy pot. Attach a deep-fry thermometer and heat the oil over medium-high heat to bring the temperature to 350°F. Meanwhile, prepare a sheet tray or platter with paper towels. Working in batches, carefully submerge 2 or 3 empanadas at a time into the hot oil. Fry, while moving the empanadas continuously in the oil using a slotted spoon or metal spider, to maintain the even temperature of the oil, until golden and crispy all around, about 3 minutes. Transfer the empanadas to the prepared tray. Cover with foil and keep warm, or serve as you go.

To Bake

Preheat the oven to 375°F.

Brush each empanada with the egg wash and bake until crisp and golden, 20 to 25 minutes. Serve with the Ají de Maní and lime wedges.

PIPIÁN FILLING

MAKES 1 QUART

1 tablespoon canola oil

1 tablespoon ground achiote or sweet paprika

2 scallions, white and green parts, finely chopped

1 white onion, chopped (1¼ cups)

3 garlic cloves, grated or finely chopped

5 ripe plum tomatoes, grated or chopped (1¾ cups)

1 small red bell pepper, seeded, deveined, and chopped (¾ cup)

1 cup beef broth

¾ cup roasted unsalted peanuts, finely chopped

1 pound Yukon Gold potatoes, scrubbed and quartered

2 teaspoons kosher salt

Freshly ground black pepper

Heat the oil in a large skillet over medium heat. Add the achiote, scallions, and onion and sauté, stirring with a wooden spoon, until the onion softens without browning, 3 to 4 minutes. Add the garlic, tomatoes, and bell pepper, and stir to incorporate. Continue cooking until the vegetables begin to soften and form a sauce, 4 to 5 minutes. Add the broth, peanuts, and potatoes and fold them into the bubbling sauce. Season with the salt and pepper to taste, cover, and cook over medium-low heat—checking every now and then to make sure the ingredients don't dry out—until the potatoes begin to fall apart, 25 to 28 minutes. Turn off the heat, uncover, and set aside to cool.

AJÍ DE MANÍ

MAKES 1½ CUPS

1 cup dry-roasted salted peanuts

2 ripe plum tomatoes, grated (including skins and seeds)

1 hard-boiled egg, finely chopped

1 bird's eye chili, chopped (seeded and deveined if you prefer less heat)

2 tablespoons white vinegar

½ teaspoon kosher salt

Place the peanuts, tomatoes, egg, chili, vinegar, and salt into a food processor, and blend until smooth. Add a few tablespoons of water at a time to make the consistency spoonable but not too runny.

¾ cup long-grain white rice, soaked in water for at least 12 hours, drained

¾ cup yuca flour

1 large egg

1½ pounds grated Cotija cheese

1 teaspoon baking powder

½ cup cold water

PANDEBONOS

RICE BREAD PUFFS

The legendary salsa band Grupo Niche dedicated a song to the city of Cali and its end of the year festivities. The song is called "Ají" and at one point in it, the chorus declares that *"esto es cuestión de Pandebono,"* "This is a matter of Pandebono." Sensical or not, I find in this phrase a charming analogy: any situation can be solved in a simple way. It can be something as simple as a *pandebono*, the puffy, salty, and deliciously chewy pastry that resembles its Brazilian cousin, the *pao de queijo* (cheese bread). I make them pretty small, especially when they are meant to be an appetizer.

Preheat the oven to 400°F. Line two baking sheets with parchment paper.

Place the drained rice in the bowl of a food processor and pulse until it forms a very fine powder. Transfer into a large bowl. Add the yuca flour, egg, cheese, and baking powder. Stir to combine. Pour in the cold water and knead to form a dough. You may need to add a couple tablespoons of extra water if the dough feels dry.

With your hands wet—this is paramount, otherwise the dough sticks to one's hands, falling apart—shape pieces of dough into 40 bite-size balls and place on the prepared baking sheets about 1 inch apart. Bake for 20 to 25 minutes, until golden brown.

Serve warm.

Tip: Pandebonos can be frozen prior to baking and can go straight from freezer to oven; simply add 10 minutes to the baking time.

3 pounds lean brisket

3 pounds beef back ribs, fat cap removed

3 pounds pork ribs

Kosher salt

Freshly ground black pepper

3 garlic cloves, grated

4 tablespoons canola oil, divided

5 ripe plum tomatoes, grated

6 large scallions, white and light green parts only, chopped (2 cups)

2 yellow onions, chopped

1 yuca, peeled and cut into 1-inch pieces (14 to 16 ounces)

2 large green plantains, peeled and cut into 2-inch-thick rounds

½ bunch cilantro, both stems and leaves

20 small Yukon Gold potatoes, scrubbed

4 large ears corn, shucked and cut crosswise into 2-inch pieces

4 to 6 cups white rice (recipe follows)

4 ripe avocados, cut into wedges

Ají (page 145)

4 juicy limes, cut in half (optional)

SANCOCHO

BEEF, PORK & VEGETABLE STEW

This is the ultimate one-pot meal that feeds many and comforts all. By far, my favorite traditional main course. Essentially a soup made with meat (a combination of beef and pork) or seafood and root vegetables, the dish varies from home to home and town to town.

A whole book could be written about this dish, since it has been adapted and appropriated by many countries across Latin America and the Caribbean. Hence, *sancocho* recipes are personal, unscripted, often use locally available ingredients , and can be watered down if unexpected mouths show up.

Serving and eating *sancocho* is particularly personal. I go with how it was always served at my mother's home: Once the soup is ready, the roots, corn, and meats are taken out of the broth and divided onto large platters. The broth is then strained, skimmed, and reheated to be served on the side along with lime wedges, avocado slices, white rice, and ají.

Each person gets a plate and a bowl, and they assemble their own *sancocho* as they wish. Some cut the roots and meats up to add back into the broth, while others eat it separately and sip the broth between bites. Whichever way you choose is fine.

Regardless, there is a lot of silverware involved.

Rinse the brisket, beef ribs, and pork ribs, and pat dry. Season liberally with salt and pepper and rub with the grated garlic. Allow the meats to marinate for at least 30 minutes as you prep the vegetables and make the *guiso* (tomato and onion base), which is the pillar to flavor the soup.

Heat 2 tablespoons of the canola oil in a medium skillet over low heat. Add the tomatoes, scallions, and onions and cook, stirring, until the vegetables soften and the juices thicken slightly, 8 to 9 minutes. Remove from the heat, season with salt and pepper, and set aside.

In a large soup pot, heat the remaining 2 tablespoons oil over medium-high heat, and in batches, sear the meats until golden brown, 5 to 7 minutes per side, without moving them in between turns. Once all the meats are seared, return the brisket, beef ribs, and pork ribs to the pot. Cover with water, add the tomato and onion *guiso*, and simmer covered for 1½ to 2 hours. Check the meats for tenderness—the ribs will still adhere to the bone but a bit more tender. Add the yuca, plantains, and cilantro and cook for 25 to 30 minutes. Add the potatoes and corn and simmer until the potatoes are tender but still hold their shape, 20 to 25 minutes.

This is the ideal moment to get the rice going (recipe follows).

Taste for salt and adjust the seasoning.

Remove the vegetables and meat from the broth and add to serving platters. I like serving the plantains, potatoes, yuca, and corn separately from the meat. Cut the ribs off the bones and the brisket into chunks. Skim any fat off the broth—cooling it a bit makes it easier to have a clear soup. Discard the cilantro stems.

Reheat the broth. Serve in a soup terrine or ladle directly into bowls. Accompany the soup with the meat, vegetables, rice, avocado, and ají. I love adding a squeeze of lime right before devouring.

SERVES 10 TO 12

3 cups long-grain white rice

1 tablespoon canola oil

6 cups water

2 teaspoons kosher salt

ARROZ BLANCO

White Rice

Wash the rice under cold water and drain. Repeat until the water runs clear.

Heat the oil in a heavy-bottom medium pot over medium-high heat and add the rice. Stir the rice into the oil using a wooden spoon, so that all the grains get coated by the oil, 30 to 45 seconds. Pour in the water and season with the salt. Bring to a boil and cook, uncovered, until almost all the water evaporates and the top of the rice begins to surface. Lower the heat to low and cover. Cook until the rice is tender, 18 to 20 minutes. Fluff the rice using a fork, cover, and keep warm until ready to serve.

Dessert

SERVES 8 TO 10

2 teaspoons extra-virgin olive oil

5 medium organic limes, zested and juiced (¼ cup zest, ½ cup juice)

5 large organic eggs, whites and yolks separated

⅓ cup sugar, divided

2¼ teaspoons plain gelatin or 1 envelope Knox gelatin

¼ cup cold water

½ cup sweetened condensed milk

¼ teaspoon kosher salt

3 tablespoons aged rum

ESPONJADO DE LIMÓN

LIME MOUSSE

The Cauca Valley region is filled with citrus groves that perfume the air. Aroma has the power to transport. I still remember how the smell of lime zest seemed to magically take me one day from the test kitchen at *Gourmet* all the way to my aunt Guiomar's home in Colombia.

Esponjados, or mousses using gelatin, eggs, cream, and fruit, are a very common dessert all over the country, especially in warm weather regions like the Cauca Valley. This mousse is light, airy, and the perfect ending to a large meal.

Grease a 10-cup metal or glass bowl with the olive oil and sprinkle the lime zest over the surface to coat evenly.

In a clean medium metal bowl, whisk the egg whites with a hand mixer to form stiff peaks. Slowly add the sugar with the motor running until the whites are nice and glossy. Set aside.

In a small bowl, dissolve the gelatin in the water and set aside to bloom.

In a separate bowl, whisk the yolks on high speed until the mixture is pale yellow and creamy, 5 to 7 minutes. Pour in the sweetened condensed milk, add the salt, and whisk to incorporate.

Place the gelatin, which should now be firm and gummy, into the microwave for 30 seconds at a time to dissolve.

Pour the gelatin into the yolk mixture along with the rum and lime juice and stir to incorporate completely.

With a rubber spatula, fold half of the egg whites into the yolk and gelatin mixture until they are completely incorporated. Fold in the remaining whites and pour the mousse into the prepared bowl.

Refrigerate for at least 2 hours. To serve, scoop into small plates.

The mousse will keep, covered with plastic wrap and refrigerated, for up to 3 days.

CACHACO COOL

Early in the morning, a thick fog rolls over Bogotá's savanna. The grass looks white from the frozen morning dew and the eucalyptus-lined country roads lead to the outskirts of the city with sprawling dairy and flower farms. At 8,500 feet above sea level, this place is the land of strawberries and cream spooned over crisp meringue—very European, one might think. It is no coincidence that people from the capital, in the center of the country, are often caricatured as women and men with snobbish airs of European aristocracy, colloquially called *cachacos*, and pictured in three-piece suits, trench coats, wool twill skirts, hats, and large black umbrellas hooked over the arm. The expression *cachaco*, according to the semiologist Armando Silva, comes from the union or the words *cachet* and *coat*. Essentially a person who wears their coat in style.

Even though social divisions established during colonial times still affect the country's capital, an *ajiáco* will be served by most families and traditional restaurants in this part of Colombia. Whether it is surrounded by Spanish tiles and old brick fireplaces, or in more humble households, the *ajiáco* soup has earned center stage in the heart of all Bogotánians.

This is a great meal for a crisp autumn day. Sit outside, in the chilly air under a sunny sky, sipping on *refajo* (a beer cocktail) and snacking on bites of spicy radishes. The table is set inside, the fireplace is roaring, and *ajiáco* will soon be served.

Cocktail

REFAJO A LA BROOKLYN
Aperol, Beer & Orange Spritz

Starter

RÁBANOS Y VERDURAS CON SAL
Radishes & Veggies Dipped in Salt

Main

BOGOTÁNIAN AJIÁCO
Potato Soup with Corn, Chicken & Capers

Dessert

MERENGÓN DE FRESA Y CREMA DE DIENTE DE LEON
Strawberry Meringue with Dandelion Cream

SETTING THE SCENE

Carnations are the most undervalued flower of all time. The trick is quantity—clustered together in tiny short vases or giant amphoras filled with bundles, they make a statement. Avoid the flimsy stems that are cut too long. Pick your color and stay within that palette. Look for the large variety rather than the small skinny ones.

In addition, eucalyptus branches have a glorious scent, are quite inexpensive, and last a long time; I love incorporating varieties like silver dollar, true blue, or willow, along with a few garden roses and carnations. Keep table flowers small to give just a pop of color here and there and leave the large arrangements for the entryway, the bar, or a side table. It is lovely to find a fragrant eucalyptus branch in the bathroom as well. I am not a florist (there are incredibly talented floral artists out there who make magnificent arrangements), so I would say I am rather flexible when it comes to putting elements together in a vase. I do know I like arrangements that are loose, unfussy, and a tad disheveled.

To set the table, bring out the family china or your flea market finds and combine them with rustic earthenware.

HOW I HOST

One of the things that I missed the most while working as a line cook at Prune in New York and the Post Ranch Inn in California was dressing up for work—something you don't do if you change into a chef's coat as soon as you get to your job! So, when I began working as a food stylist and wearing my own clothes again, I designed my own aprons, which I have since turned into a line called Mariana's Limonarium. I was looking for something that would not only suit the utilitarian need of protecting my clothes from oil spatters and such, but would also look professional and, frankly, make me *feel* well dressed.

A hosting apron is what you wear when you'll invariably have to jump back to the kitchen to take the roast out of the oven or prepare the final touches. A well-designed apron gives you confidence both in and out of the kitchen. I recommend investing in one you love and are happy to wear in front of guests.

THE ART OF SEATING

The Colombian way of life is, the more the merrier. When unexpected guests turn up, don't panic. A table for 10 or 12 can easily turn into 15. Sit people as you would like the night to go. The traditional way would be girl-boy-girl, but it is about mixing it up—not only gender-wise but also by interests and connections, which is key to good conversation! Separating couples will give them their own tales to tell each other at the end of the night. Seat people together with acute interests, sensibilities, or, possibly, romantic attractions in a clandestine attempt for love. An eclectic mélange of guests with different ages, tastes, and backgrounds makes for the best dinner parties.

PLAYLIST

A cold afternoon in Bogotá feels like a fall day in New York. Turn the heat up on your *ajiáco*, chill up the *refajo*, and start it all up with these tunes.

"Fruitflies" by Gabriel Garzón-Montano
"Caviar" by Salt Cathedral
"Ocean Beach" by Black Mighty Orchestra
"Cou-Cou" by Monsieur Periné
"True Love" by Esteman / Monsieur Periné
"Show Me the Way to Go Home" by Julie London
"Moonglow" by Artie Shaw
"Blue Eyes" by Destroyer
"The Homeless Wanderer" by Emahoy Tsegué-Maryam Guèbrou
"Battez-vous" by Brigitte

Cocktail

MAKES 1

3 ounces Aperol

3 ounces orange juice

Ice

1 (6-ounce) can pilsner beer, chilled

REFAJO A LA BROOKLYN

APEROL, BEER & ORANGE SPRITZ

Officially, *refajo* is an *aperitivo* made with one part ice-cold pilsner mixed with one part soda (specifically, an orange-colored cola sold in Colombia called, of all things, Colombiana!). This mix is the classic drink of *la sabana*: light, without much alcohol, refreshing, and easy. One could compare it to an Aperol spritz or the British Pimm's and lemonade, sans the fruit.

   With all these ideas in mind, I've stirred up my own version of *refajo*. Beer, Aperol, and orange juice à la Brooklyn. Similar flavors with a different take.

Pour the Aperol and orange juice into a highball glass filled with ice, stir with a long spoon, and top off with the beer.

SERVES 8 TO 10

30 small radishes,
any variety

2 bunches asparagus,
trimmed and cut into
2-inch pieces

3 heads endive,
leaves removed

½ cup flaky sea salt,
such as Maldon

RÁBANOS Y VERDURAS CON SAL

RADISHES & VEGGIES DIPPED IN SALT

Serving whole radishes and other veggies with their leaves attached, accompanied by a little bowl of sea salt, is a signature part of my entertaining style. The radishes look especially gorgeous on platters, and the only prep work needed is a good wash and a trim of any dead leaves. I get my radishes from the farmers market—the bunches are large and inexpensive and there is a chance to get beautiful varieties such as the long and skinny French breakfast radish or the purple and pink Easter egg radish.

Wash the radishes well, as they tend to be rather sandy when coming from the farmers market. Remove any bad leaves and keep a nice top of two or three leaves attached. Plunge the radishes into a bowl of very cold water to crisp up and to give the extra dirt a chance to sink down to the bottom. Do the same with the asparagus, endive, and any other vegetables of your choice.

When ready to serve, lift the vegetables from the water, shake them a bit, and place wet—this will make the salt stick—onto a large platter with the salt on the side.

SERVES 8 TO 10

2 pounds russet
potatoes, peeled and cut
into ¼-inch-thick rounds

1 pound Criolla potatoes
or gold creamer potatoes,
peeled and sliced into
¼-inch-thick rounds

1½ pounds large Yukon Gold
potatoes, peeled and sliced
into ¼-inch-thick rounds

3 pounds bone-in chicken
breasts, skin removed

2 teaspoons kosher salt

Freshly ground black pepper

4 whole large scallions,
trimmed

3 garlic cloves, peeled
and smashed

3 cilantro stems, whole

5 ears corn, husked, silky
threads removed, each cut
into 3 to 4 pieces

10 grams dried *guasca*

1½ cups heavy cream

1 cup large capers

3 to 4 ripe avocados, cut into
wedges right before serving

BOGOTÁNIAN AJIÁCO

POTATO SOUP WITH CORN, CHICKEN & CAPERS

This soup was declared cultural patrimony by the mayor's office in Bogotá about twenty years ago. Cultural patrimony is "a set of goods and values that are an expression of the people." And this soup is quite an expression of our people. It dates back to pre-Hispanic times, where one of the first recipes for *ajiáco* was based on various roots and tubers accompanied by *guascas*—an aromatic bitter green—and venison. Although it was always thought to be of Muisca origin—the native tribe of central Colombia—according to the historian Lácidez Moreno, *ajiáco* has African roots. Just like humanity.

However, to current Colombians, especially Bogotánians, there is only one true *ajiáco*—a hearty soup made with three kinds of potatoes, corn, chicken, *guasca* herbs, cream, avocado, and capers.

The three potatoes in the soup each serve a purpose. The *sabanera* potato, which I replace with russet potatoes, dissolves into the broth, giving it its creamy quality. The second potato is called *pastusa*, which gives flavor and texture. In this case I use large Yukon Golds as a substitute. Finally, to get the yellow color and sweet taste, there is the Criolla potato, which you can replace with tiny gold creamer potatoes or yellow new potatoes.

Guasca is an herb also known as galisonga for New Zealanders, or gallant soldier in Ireland—the latter naturally my favorite of its many names. In the United States, *guasca* can be found at farmers markets by the name of potato weed. This fragrant herb imparts a particular taste to *ajiáco* and can be found in dried form online or in the spice section of the few Colombian markets around the United States. However, if *guasca* is not an option, it should not be a deterrent from making this comforting recipe.

Invite another pair of hands into the kitchen to help you peel the potatoes. It will go quicker, and it is a good way to spark conversation while making lunch.

Place the russet, Criolla, and Yukon Gold potatoes, the chicken breasts, salt, pepper to taste, scallions, garlic, and cilantro in a large soup pot. Cover entirely with cold water and bring to a simmer over high heat, occasionally skimming off the foam that rises to the top. Cook at a slow simmer until the chicken breasts are cooked through but still juicy, about 45 minutes. Using tongs, lift the chicken breasts, scallions, and cilantro from the soup. Set aside the chicken breasts to cool, and discard the scallions and cilantro.

Give the soup a stir and continue cooking until the potatoes have started to dissolve and the consistency is thick and creamy, with some potato chunks remaining, 45 to 50 minutes. Turn off the heat and keep covered until right before serving.

Meanwhile, place a medium pot of salted water over high heat, bring to a boil, add the corn pieces, and bring back to a boil. Cover, turn off the heat, and leave for 10 minutes. Remove the corn and set aside to serve later.

When the chicken breasts are cool enough to handle, shred into large pieces and transfer to a serving platter. Tent with foil and keep warm.

About 10 minutes before serving the *ajiáco*, add the *guasca*. Heat back up over medium heat, stirring often with a wooden spoon to keep from burning at the bottom.

Ladle into bowls and serve with the chicken, heavy cream, capers, and avocado slices on the side.

Dessert

SERVES 10 TO 12

For the meringue

6 egg whites, at
room temperature

2 cups superfine sugar

2 tablespoons pure
vanilla extract

1 tablespoon cornstarch

1 teaspoon white vinegar

For the cream

2 cups chilled heavy cream

1½ teaspoons dandelion
bitters or Angostura bitters

2 pounds small ripe
strawberries, hulled
and halved

2 tablespoons lemon juice

2 teaspoons superfine sugar

Dandelion petals,
for garnish (optional)

MERENGÓN DE FRESA Y CREMA DE DIENTE DE LEÓN

STRAWBERRY SHEET MERINGUE WITH DANDELION CREAM

A large white banner reading MERENGÓN DE FRESA stretches between makeshift poles on the side of the road along the Bogotá savanna. Past the sign, a boxy Renault 12—a French-made car brought to our country in the 1970s—sits with its lights on and its trunk propped open, displaying trays of crunchy meringue topped with whipped cream and strawberries. The *merengón* is sold by families who prepare this dessert during the week and venture to country roads on the weekend to sell to passersby. It's a less refined pavlova, but with all its decadence.

In this version, I take all the richness of a Renault 12 *merengón* and add a dash of dandelion bitters to bring to mind the yellow flowers that blanket the fields of the area.

Preheat the oven to 200°F.

Line an 11 x 17-inch baking sheet with parchment paper.

Pour the egg whites into the clean bowl of an electric mixer fitted with the whisk attachment. Mix on low speed for 10 to 15 seconds to loosen up the egg whites. Gradually increase the speed until the egg whites are light and foamy. Slowly add the sugar, 1 tablespoon at a time, and continue mixing on high speed until the meringue is glossy and stiff peaks form, 4 to 5 minutes. Add the vanilla, cornstarch, and vinegar and mix a few more seconds to incorporate. Using a rubber spatula, gently transfer the meringue onto the prepared baking sheet and spread to form a rectangle. Transfer to the oven and bake until slightly golden and set, 55 to 60 minutes. Remove from the oven and cool.

In the meantime, prepare the cream: Place the metal bowl of a stand mixer and the whisk attachment in the freezer for at least 10 minutes.

Remove the chilled bowl and whisk attachment from the freezer, pour in the cream and bitters, and whisk on medium speed until soft peaks form, about 2 minutes. Transfer the whipped cream to a separate bowl and refrigerate until ready to assemble.

Place the strawberries, lemon juice, and sugar into a medium bowl and stir to combine. Allow the berries to macerate for at least 15 minutes.

Assemble the *merengón*: Transfer the baked meringue onto a large platter. Spread the cream all over the surface, leaving about a ½-inch border, pizza style. Scatter the strawberries and drizzle their juices over the cream and garnish with the dandelion petals, if using.

Cut into messy squares and serve.

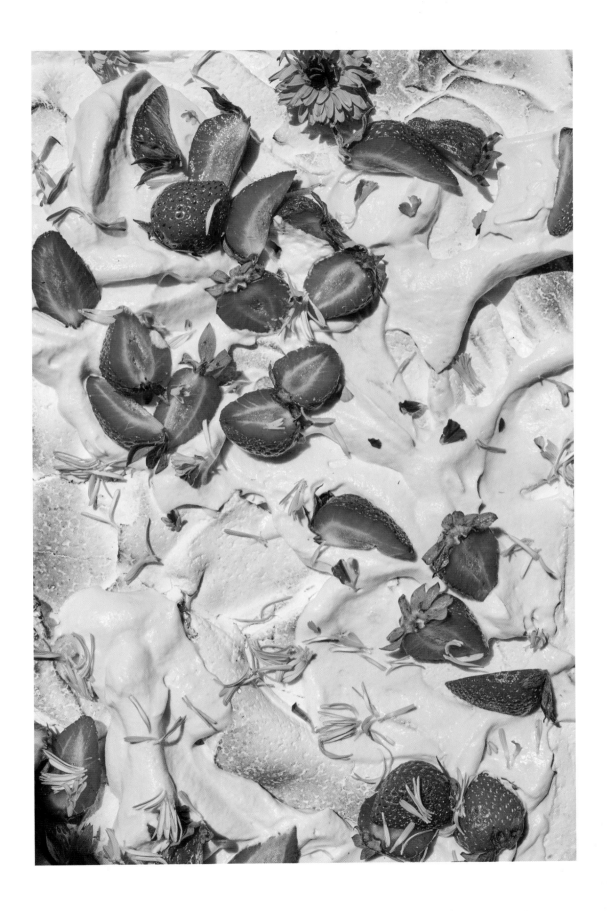

MEDELLÍN'S ONLY SEASON

The weather: a balmy 70 degrees. The yellow *guayacán* trees are in constant bloom. The region is Antioquia, the vertiginous Andes' western mountain range famous for its industrious habitants, most of whom live in or near Medellín, a town where it is spring all year long.

The quintessential Medellín attitude is perfectly depicted in one woman whose name gives title to a great Colombian novel, *The Marchioness of Yolombó* (Carrasquilla, 1928). Imaginary or real, this marchioness was a strong woman who rejected colonial social norms and insisted on working in her father's gold mine from the age of seven. She befriended slaves and workers. Four years later, she was able to build schools for low-income children, becoming a cultural patron, advocate against slavery, and supporter of Afro-Colombian and indigenous rights.

In essence, the marchioness represents the power and persuasive determination of all women in her region and of us Colombianas.

Today, art deco buildings contrast with the two-story farmhouses that have bright-colored wooden wrap-around balconies, perched on the hills of endless coffee plantations. This typical Antioquian country home, with hanging baskets of anthuriums, rustic furniture, and simple checkered tablecloths, is the heart of *frijolada*, a traditional lunch made with stewed beans, *chicharrón*, rice, arepas, sweet plantains, and avocado.

I envision this meal being served over a vintage tablecloth with handmade black ceramic bowls from those little towns in the surrounding areas, and their matching soup terrine holding the piping hot red beans.

Cocktail

MISTELA DE MORA
Blackberry Mistela with Green Pepper & Bay

Starter

AREPITAS CON JALEA DE TOMATE Y CORIANDRO
Grilled Arepitas & Tomato Coriander Jam

Main

FRÍJOLES CON CARNE EN POLVO, CHICHARRÓN, MADUROS, ARROZ BLANCO Y AJÍ
Red Bean Soup with Brisket Dust, Pork Belly, Sweet Plantains, White Rice & Ají

Dessert

NIEVE DE "CAFÉ CON LECHE" Y SUSPIROS DE CACAO
"Café con Leche" Granita with Tiny Cocoa Meringues

SETTING THE SCENE

Hand-painted earthenware is making a comeback. More and more contemporary makers are rescuing ancient traditions in tableware around the world, from Japanese porcelains to Oaxacan pottery. I personally love organic shapes, textured materials, and objects with stories. This is why our table is set with hand-painted plates from a town in the region of Antioquia called El Carmen de Viboral, known as the cradle of artisanal ceramics, where many families and makers create this emblematic floral dining ware; vintage salt and pepper shakers that take us back to the kitschy details of coffee plantations; and checkered tablecloths that elevate an earnest tone, classic to the Paisa culture. Add a scattering of bright red flowers such as anthuriums here and there, and a soup terrine to keep beans hot alongside mismatched serving platters to set the perfect mood.

HOW I HOST

At home, my husband and I host together. We each have a set of tasks that, with time, have become a source of pride for both of us. It is the part we play in the art of entertaining. To me it is a tribute, a dance, a way to show appreciation and care for those who come over.

Diego makes well-thought-out playlists, sets up the bar, gets ice from the deli, receives coats, and pours the first drink, while I run around the kitchen and table—always barefoot—until the first time the buzzer goes off and the first guests show up.

Before I got married, living in a tiny Manhattan apartment where I had an electric stove and a kitchen with no counter space, I would host dinners all the time and I kept it all very simple. I either recruited some friends who love to cook to bring a few things to lighten my load, such as dessert, an appetizer, or a cheese board—which also made them feel included and trusted. Or I would buy some good-quality premade hors d'oeuvres, which I still sometimes do. Finding and trying out brands for, say, frozen empanadas, mini tamales, a great paté, or a smoked fish salad can take care of part of the meal, leaving you with just the main course. Having to do it all is too much pressure. With these menus I hope to inspire feasts by sharing all the recipes, but by all means, mix and match. Serve ice cream or ice pops for dessert if you want.

If someone asks to help, please let them. Hand a bottle of wine and the opener to a friend, while asking another to pass around the *arepitas*. If having a guest clearing plates as you open the dishwasher and organize a bit allows for you to get back to the table faster, please do! There is no shame in sharing the ritual of hosting.

PLAYLIST

A city known for its reggaeton also has a musical past in tango and bolero, genres that are just as heartfelt as its food.

"Jungle Dreams "by Xavier Cugat and His Waldorf-Astoria Orchestra
"Jalousie" by Esquivel
"Ladyfingers" by Herb Alpert & The Tijuana Brass
"Volver" by Carlos Gardel
"Capullito de Aleli" by Los Tres Ases
"Vereda Tropica" by Toña la Negra
"Camarera del Amor" by Benny Moré
"Dos Gardenias" by Buena Vista Social Club
"Me Lo Dijo Adela (Sweet and Gentle)" by Machito and His Afro-Cuban Orchestra
"Sólamente una Vez" by Agustín Lara

Cocktail

MAKES ABOUT 15 SERVINGS

2 bottles (750 ml per bottle) aguardiente

4 cups blackberries, washed

1 tablespoon whole green peppercorns or black peppercorns

3 fresh bay leaves

Ice

Club soda

MISTELA DE MORA

BLACKBERRY MISTELA

Aguardiente is the national liqueur of Colombia. Made from distilled sugar-cane and anís, it is prepared with pride and is a favorite ingredient for our cocktails. This recipe is essentially an infusion of fruit, spices, and Aguardiente. I chose blackberry here in remembrance of the thorny berry bush that climbed the white brick wall of my grandparents' backyard. As kids, we would pull sweater sleeves down to the tips of our fingers to be able to insert an entire arm through the prickly vines to gather the sour berries. To layer the flavors a bit I added green peppercorns and fresh bay leaves, imparting fresh and spicy tones to this drink.

Pour the *aguardiente* into a large clean mason jar or bottle with a tight seal. Add the berries, peppercorns, and bay leaves and seal. The *mistela* will be ready to drink after 3 to 5 days. Store for up to 2 weeks in a dark place or pantry, then strain and refrigerate.

Serve over ice with a splash of club soda.

MAKES 30 MINI AREPAS

Arepa dough
(see page 30)
Canola oil

AREPITAS CON JALEA DE TOMATE Y CORIANDRO

GRILLED AREPITAS & TOMATO CORIANDER JAM

Often associated just with breakfast, these charred and steamy two-bite arepas, slathered with sweet and savory jam, are a delicious appetizer. Serve them on a tray with the jam on the side.

Make the *arepitas*: Line a baking sheet with parchment paper and set aside. Form 30 balls with the dough and then flatten each ball with your hands, smoothing the edges with your fingers. Each *arepita* should be around ½ inch thick. Place the small *arepitas* on the prepared baking sheet and set aside.

Preheat the oven to 325°F.

Heat 2 tablespoons oil or a coating of cooking spray in a large cast-iron grill pan over medium heat. Add the *arepitas* to the pan without overcrowding (about 10), and cook for 4 to 5 minutes on each side until they are cooked through and have nice golden brown marks. Use a spatula to turn them over. Set aside on a baking sheet and place in the warm oven. Repeat, adding 2 tablespoons of oil per batch.

MAKES 1 CUP

1 (14-ounce) can peeled canned tomatoes

1 teaspoon achiote powder or sweet paprika

2 large garlic cloves, roughly chopped

2 to 3 tablespoons coriander seeds, toasted

½ teaspoon fine sea salt

¼ teaspoon freshly ground black pepper

2 tablespoons extra-virgin olive oil

TOMATO CORIANDER JAM

My life changed the day I tasted the tomato magic made by Paula Wolfert for her cookbook *The Food of Morocco*, which I styled in Marrakesh back in 2011. Her sweet, jammy tomato compote was so simple, yet so addictive. I adapted Wolfert's recipe by exchanging Middle Eastern spices for *achiote* and coriander seeds—the seeds sprinkled on top of the steaming golden arepas.

In a food processor or blender, combine the canned tomatoes and the juice with the achiote powder, garlic cloves, coriander seeds, salt, pepper, and olive oil. Puree until smooth.

Transfer to a wide, heavy-bottom saucepan and set over medium-low heat. Cook slowly, stirring often, until the tomato mixture reduces to a thick jam, 25 to 30 minutes.

Let the mixture cool completely, then pour into a clean glass jar and seal with a lid. The jam can be stored in the refrigerator for up to 10 days.

To serve, top the *arepitas* with 1 teaspoon of the jam and arrange on a serving platter. Alternatively, place the jam into a decorative bowl and serve alongside the *arepitas*.

SERVES 8 TO 10

1 pound dried red beans,
soaked overnight

1 pound pumpkin, peeled

4 medium carrots, peeled

2½ quarts water

1 tablespoon extra-virgin
olive oil

1 red onion,
roughly chopped

4 garlic cloves

½ bunch fresh cilantro,
stems included

1 small red bell pepper,
seeded, deveined, and
roughly chopped

4 teaspoons fine sea salt,
plus more as needed

FRÍJOLES CON CARNE EN POLVO, CHICHARRÓN, MADUROS, ARROZ BLANCO Y AJÍ

RED BEAN SOUP WITH BRISKET DUST, PORK BELLY, SWEET PLANTAINS, WHITE RICE & AJÍ

This is the Antioquian region's core dish, a stewy preparation of soupy red beans with pork accompanied by sweet plantains, avocado, white rice, and powdered ground brisket. Its name: *frijolada*. My dear friend Natalia—native of Medellín, chef extraordinaire, and one of the most authentic people I know—helped me develop this recipe based on her family's Sunday lunch tradition. Soaking the beans overnight makes the cooking process faster. If you don't have a pressure cooker, simply double the cooking time.

Drain the pre-soaked beans and wash thoroughly. Place the beans in a pressure cooker along with the pumpkin, carrots, water, and oil. Cover the pressure cooker with the lid, making sure it's closed properly. Cook the beans on high heat for 20 minutes to start softening the beans. Turn off and very carefully let all the steam vent.

Open the lid and remove the pumpkin and carrots and place them in a blender along with the red onion, garlic, cilantro, red bell pepper, and 1 cup of the cooking liquid from the beans. Blend until you have a smooth puree. Pour the puree back into the pressure cooker, add the salt, and cover again. Cook over high heat for 10 minutes, remove from the heat, and carefully let the steam escape before you remove the pressure cooker cover. Place the uncovered pressure cooker back on the stove over medium-high heat until the beans reach a simmer. Let simmer for 25 to 30 minutes, until the liquid thickens. Season with more salt if needed.

Serve the beans in a large soup terrine. Set the table with soup bowls for the soupy beans and dinner plates. Accompany with the following sides served in trays and bowls so that everyone can make their own plate.

Brisket Dust (*Carne en Polvo*, recipe follows)

Sweet Plantains (*Maduros*, recipe follows on page 144)

Ají (recipe follows on page 145)

White Rice (*Arroz Blanco*, page 113)

Crispy Pork Belly (recipe follows on page 145)

3 ripe Hass avocados, pitted, peeled, and sliced into spears

SERVES 8 TO 10
(MAKES 5½ CUPS)

2½ pounds brisket,
 cut into cubes

1 tablespoon kosher salt

1 red onion, quartered

2 whole scallions, trimmed

8 cilantro sprigs,
including stems

8 garlic cloves, smashed

1 small red bell pepper,
seeded, deveined, and
roughly chopped

CARNE EN POLVO

BRISKET DUST

Salt the brisket generously.

Place the brisket, onion, scallions, cilantro sprigs, garlic, and bell pepper into a medium Dutch oven and add water to cover by 2 inches. Bring to a boil over high heat , then lower the heat to medium and cover. Simmer the brisket, checking now and then to ensure the heat is consistent (not too low nor at a rapid boil), until the meat is tender and the fibers easily pull away, 2 to 2½ hours.

If you have a pressure cooker or Instant Pot, place the brisket, onion, scallions, cilantro sprigs, garlic, and bell pepper into the pot and add water to cover by 2 inches. Cover with the lid and cook, following the manufacturer's instructions, at high pressure for 40 minutes. Turn the heat off and let all the steam escape before opening the lid. Drain the meat and vegetables into a large metal colander, setting inside a large bowl to catch the dripping broth. Discard the vegetables and allow the meat to cool in the colander, about 20 minutes.

When the meat is at room temperature, transfer to a food processor and process to a powder, using a rubber spatula to scrape the sides once or twice. (If using a high-speed blender, cover with the lid and use the tamper.) This will take about 3 minutes. Place in a serving bowl.

MADUROS

SWEET PLANTAINS

4 large ripe plantains, peeled

3 tablespoons sunflower oil

Sea salt

Slice each plantain into 6 thick slices on the bias.

Cover a large plate with paper towels. Set aside.

Heat 1 tablespoon of the oil in a medium cast-iron skillet over medium heat. Add 6 slices of plantain to the skillet and cook for 3 to 4 minutes per side, until nicely browned; watch the plantains closely, as their sugar may cause them to brown fast.

Using a spatula, remove the plantains from the skillet and place on a serving plate. Sprinkle with salt to taste. Repeat the process until you have cooked all the plantain slices.

AJÍ

MAKES 2 CUPS

1 bunch cilantro with stems, finely chopped

4 jalapeños, seeded, deveined, and finely chopped

4 *ají dulce* or 2 small red bell peppers, seeded, deveined, and finely chopped

8 scallions, white and green parts, finely chopped

2 teaspoons kosher salt

½ teaspoon freshly ground black pepper

6 tablespoons white vinegar

Juice of 1 lime

1 teaspoon red pepper flakes (optional)

The mother sauce of my country. Jars of this green, sour, and spicy condiment sit at the center of the table to be dolloped and drizzled over just about any dish.

Mix the cilantro, jalapeños, *ají dulce*, scallions, salt, black pepper, vinegar, lime juice, and red pepper flakes in a medium-size bowl. Cover with plastic wrap and let rest for 30 minutes to allow the ingredients to release their liquid and meld together.

Transfer the ají to a glass jar and store in the fridge for up to 10 days.

CHICHARRÓN

CRISPY PORK BELLY

SERVES 8 TO 10

2-pound piece pork belly, skin on

2 tablespoons kosher salt

3 limes, cut into wedges, to serve

Pat the pork belly dry using paper towels. With a sharp knife, cut it into 2-inch squares. Season with the salt and set aside. Place a Dutch oven or *caldero* over medium heat. Place the pork belly pieces skin side down and cook, undisturbed, for at least 20 minutes, until the fat begins to render. The goal is to get a crispy skin. Carefully rotate the pieces and cook for about 40 minutes longer, so that they brown on all sides. This process will take some patience, but the key is to not rush the cooking. You want as much fat out of the meat so that it is crispy and delicious. Serve warm or at room temperature with lime wedges.

SERVES 8 TO 10

"Café con Leche" Granita

2 tablespoons instant espresso

3 cups boiling water, divided

½ cup ground panela

1 teaspoon ground cardamom

½ teaspoon ground cinnamon

½ cup heavy cream

MAKES 36 MERINGUES

6 egg whites, at room temperature

½ teaspoon cream of tartar

1 cup superfine sugar

½ teaspoon kosher salt

1 tablespoon pure vanilla extract

½ cup unsweetened cocoa powder

NIEVE DE "CAFÉ CON LECHE" Y SUSPIROS DE CACAO

"CAFÉ CON LECHE" GRANITA WITH TINY COCOA MERINGUES

Despite my love for coffee, I have never been a fan of coffee-flavored desserts. In this sense I am a purist: coffee is best served sugarless, with a little something sweet on the side. I take my morning coffee black and in the afternoon with a dash of milk. All that said, because I too have my contradictions, a coffee granita–drizzled swirl of cream is actually a perfect digestive-like dessert: fluffy coffee and cream ice served layered in a glass or cup with mini cocoa anise cookies.

In a liquid measuring cup, dissolve the instant espresso in 2 cups of the boiling water. In a large bowl, dissolve the *panela* in the remaining 1 cup boiling water. Pour the espresso into the *panela*, and mix well. Add the cardamom and cinnamon, and stir to combine.

Pour into a 9 x 9-inch metal pan and freeze for 2 hours. Smash, break up, and scrape into chunks and powder using a fork. Drizzle in the heavy cream unevenly and freeze for 30 minutes. Serve in short clear glasses or cups alongside the tiny cocoa meringues (recipe follows).

SUSPIROS DE CACAO
Tiny Cocoa Meringues

You can use store-bought or make your own meringues. In some places, the literal translation of meringues in Spanish is *suspiros*, or sighs. This alone is enough reason for me to make my own.

Preheat the oven to 200°F. Line 2 baking sheets with parchment paper.

Place the egg whites and cream of tartar in a clean metal bowl. Begin whisking slowly with a handheld mixer (or use a stand mixer), increasing the speed little by little. When the whites begin to become fluffy, slowly add the sugar and salt as you continue mixing on high speed until the meringue is glossy and holds a nice stiff peak. Using a rubber spatula, fold in the vanilla and cocoa powder. I like not mixing the cocoa in entirely, leaving streaks of chocolaty powder in the white meringue (I personally think this looks better!). With two small spoons, shape small dollops of meringue and place about 1 inch apart on the prepared baking sheets. They don't have to be perfect, so no need to bother with using a piping bag—unless you want to. The cocoa swirls will be organic and uneven. Bake for 2 hours and remove from the oven.

The meringues will keep up to two weeks stored in a tightly sealed container.

FROM BEIRUT TO SINCELEJO

Two mango trees, one by the front entrance and the other on the back patio. The first, a sign of welcome. The second, a source of shade for what was essentially my grandmother Lola's living room. This black and white tiled patio was home to every part of life—sitting down to family meals, reading the newspaper, entertaining guests. A white forged-iron dining table and two wooden rocking chairs surrounded by lush ferns and vines made the patio feel classic, yet ageless. This is the magic of Middle Eastern–style architecture brought to the Sinú River Valley by immigrants like my father's Syrian-Lebanese family, who arrived in Colombia in the late nineteenth and early twentieth centuries.

Migration and the evolution of cuisine go hand-in-hand. As they deepened their roots into this new land, Middle Eastern migrants shared their stuffed fig leaves and tabbouleh, and served their bulgur and parsley salads alongside egg arepas and yuca fritters—*carimañolas*. Two cuisines became one. As the Lebanese-Colombian journalist-writer Juan Gossain once wrote, "I am the legitimate son of a *quippe* and an egg arepa."

I believe I am their daughter.

This mélange of cultures and flavors only grew richer with the passage of time. Allspice and sesame, mixed with corn and plantains, are now staples on the northern coast. Sweet layers of phyllo dough and honeyed nuts from Damascus now share trays with mango jellies and sweetened tamarind balls.

Such a feast is meant to be savored slowly, like the rhythm of Arab poems or the harvest of apricots in spring. The meal starts with a tray of mezze served casually for guests to nibble as they please—*quippe* or *kibbe* made of ground beef, bulgur, and pine nuts; *carimañolas*—yuca fritters filled with cheese or meat; marinated olives; and a watercress and purslane lemony salad. A refreshing coconut rum *aperitivo* helps the humid afternoon go by more pleasurably.

Later, lunch is served: *mote* soup is gently ladled into bowls, topped with eggplant slices and accompanied by watercress salad at the center of the table.

Cocktail

COQUITO
Mío Rum & Coconut Cocktail

Starter

CARIMAÑOLAS CON CARNE Y SUERO Stuffed Yuca Fritters with Crème Fraîche
Olives
Hummus
Warmed pita bread

Main

ENSALADA DE BERROS Y LIMÓN Lemony Watercress Salad
MOTE DE QUESO DE LA NIÑA LOLA Creamy Yam Soup with Cheese

Dessert

ALASKA DE MANGO Y AJONJOLÍ Mango Sesame Baked Alaska

SETTING THE SCENE

For this meal I like to use indigo and patterned earthenware, mixed printed linens, and short glasses. The flowers can be muted to contrast with the prints—pale pink anthuriums with some gray or beige foliage for texture.

I have a tradition of placing a little something under each dinner plate on a set table. It can be a chocolate coin, a paper fish, or a personal message. I was evidently inspired by fortune cookies and their little treat of information. Once the savory part of the meal is over and plates are taken off the table, it offers a fun and surprising treat.

HOW I HOST

After a long meal at the table, changing things up is a must. Not only so that people's conversations can stay lively, and limbs stretched, but also because a change of space for dessert will ease in the afternoon, casually extending the feast. Have dessert plates and forks/spoons ready to go on a tray. I prefer bringing dessert to the coffee table. I love kneeling or sitting low to the ground, and plating to individual desired serving size. Have a few glasses ready in case someone would like a pousse-café such as port or rum.

PLAYLIST

Follow an international musical path inspired by Syrian-Lebanese migrants who arrived in Colombia centuries ago.

"Argosvinis Moni" by Imam Baildi
"PARIS" by Salt Cathedral
"Les Tuileries" by Colette Magny
"Fiesta en Corraleja" by Billo's Caracas Boys
"Coffee Bean / Calabash Annie" by Les Baxter
"Rainbow Girl" by Lily Chao
"Tolú" by Sonido Gallo Negro
"Sólamente una Vez" by Alondra de la Parra / Agustín Lara
"Charlotte Is Dead (Thoughts of Lolita)" by Nelson Riddle
"Misirlou" by Martin Denny

Cocktail

SERVES 8

2 cups (16 ounces)
coconut water

2 cups (16 ounces)
Clément Coconut Liqueur

1 cup (8 ounces) aged rum
(La Hechicera, made in
Barranquilla, is my favorite)

5 tablespoons
(2½ ounces) lime juice

Ice

Edible flowers,
for garnish (optional)

Lime peel,
for garnish (optional)

COQUITO MIO

RUM & COCONUT COCKTAIL

Sunscreen is the scent of vacation. Although I love coconut, its common liqueurs tend to taste like… well, SPF 40. Thankfully there is a liqueur called Clément made of young coconut meat steeped in rum. The taste is clean, non-oily, and subtle—like leaving a yoga class, without the funk.

Making batch cocktails is a necessity, unless you are shaking every cocktail at your parties—more power to you if you are. Having a large batch of a deliciously tangy, sweet, buzzy beverage to begin the affair is a lovely offer.

Mix the coconut water, coconut liqueur, rum, and lime juice in a large pitcher, stir with a long spoon, and refrigerate until very, very cold. To serve, pour into ice-filled rocks glasses, or shake with lots of ice and strain into coupes.

If using, garnish with the edible flowers or a lime twist, or both!

MAKES 15 SMALL FRITTERS

For the dough

3 pounds yuca root, peeled, quartered, deveined, and cut into 2-inch chunks

2 teaspoons kosher salt

2 tablespoons canola oil, plus 4 cups (if deep-frying)

1 egg (if baking)

For the meat filling

10 ounces lean ground beef

3 garlic cloves, finely minced or grated

1 teaspoon plus a pinch of kosher salt

1 tablespoon extra-virgin olive oil

1 small onion, grated

1 tomato, grated

1 teaspoon ground achiote or sweet paprika

Freshly ground black pepper

2 teaspoons ground coriander

For the cheese filling

5 ounces (150 grams) whole-milk mozzarella cheese, cut into 1-inch x ¼-inch batons

Crème fraîche, *crema*, or *Ají* (page 145), for serving

CARIMAÑOLAS DE QUESO Y CARNE

YUCA FRITTERS STUFFED WITH CHEESE AND BEEF

These sweet and pillowy yuca bites shaped like a football and filled with either ground meat or cheese are an essential item on the *fritos* list. Starchy yuca gets cooked and mashed into a soft dough, which is then filled with a flavorful beef picadillo or a chunk of cheese, and is later deep-fried to crispy perfection. Baking is also an option, so I've included both methods.

For frying, I like using a cheese that holds its shape and gets chewy rather than melty, such as halloumi. However, a firm mozzarella also works very well.

To make the dough

Place the yuca in a medium pot, cover with cold water, and season with the salt. Bring to a boil over high heat, then lower the heat to medium-low and cook until tender but not falling apart, 25 to 30 minutes. Drain and allow the yuca to release its steam for a few minutes—you'll start to see it turning white in some areas. While still warm, puree the yuca in a food processor or using a potato masher. Add the 2 tablespoons oil and knead to incorporate. Set aside. You will have a smooth, soft, pliable dough.

While the yuca boils, prepare the meat filling. Mix the beef, garlic, and salt in a small bowl using your hands, and set aside.

Heat the olive oil in a medium skillet over medium-high heat. Add the grated onion and tomato and cook for 3 to 5 minutes, stirring with a wooden spoon. Add the reserved ground beef and break it up with a wooden spoon. Stir in the achiote and coriander. Cook until the beef is cooked through, 2 to 3 minutes. Season with a pinch of salt and pepper, or to taste.

Turn the heat off and reserve until the mixture has cooled completely.

Place the yuca dough on a clean surface and knead a few more times. Divide the dough into 15 pieces. Shape each one into a ball, flatten with the palm of your hand, and fill with 2 teaspoons of the meat filling, or one piece of cheese. Enclose the filling, pinching the outer edges together and sealing to form a torpedo shape with the filling in the center. Place in the freezer for at least 1 hour before deep-frying.

To deep-fry

Pour about 3 inches of canola oil into a medium Dutch oven or other heavy pot, enough to submerge the fritters. Attach a deep-fry thermometer to the pot and bring the temperature to 375°F over medium-high heat. Meanwhile, prepare a sheet tray or platter lined with paper towels.

A LA MESA

Continued

Place 2 or 3 *carimañolas* in the pot at a time, moving them around in the oil until they turn golden. Drain on the lined sheet tray and serve warm with crème fraîche, crema, or *ají* .

To bake

Preheat the oven to 450°F.

Line a baking sheet with parchment paper. Crack the egg into a small bowl and whisk to make an egg wash. Place the carimañolas about ½-inch apart on the tray and brush with the egg wash. Bake in the prepared oven for 15 to 18 minutes—any longer, and the cheese filling will start to ooze out.

SERVES 6 TO 8

1 large shallot, minced

½ cup lemon juice

1 tablespoon Dijon mustard

1 cup extra-virgin olive oil

1 teaspoon kosher salt

Freshly ground black pepper

3 cups purslane

3 cups watercress

½ cup pitted black olives

ENSALADA DE BERROS

LEMONY WATERCRESS SALAD

This crunchy and tangy salad adds a green touch to the appetizer tray and uses watercress and toothy purslane leaves—most commonly found during the summer at farmers' markets. A simple lemon-shallot dressing brings this salad together and can be made ahead and kept in the refrigerator at all times—it works with just about any salad, or can be drizzled over rotisserie chicken.

Whisk together the shallot, lemon juice, and mustard in a small bowl. Add the olive oil in a steady stream while whisking to incorporate and emulsify. Season with the salt and pepper to taste, and set aside.

Toss together the purslane, watercress, olives, and dressing in a large bowl. Serve.

SERVES 8 TO 10

1 tablespoon canola oil

1 medium yellow onion, finely chopped

4 medium garlic cloves, grated

5 pounds *ñame*, peeled and cut into 3-inch pieces

2 teaspoons kosher salt

1 pound *costeño* or halloumi cheese, cubed and divided

1¼ cups *suero*, crème fraîche, or sour cream

Caramelized onion and eggplant topping

1 tablespoon olive oil

2 large yellow onions, thinly sliced

1 medium eggplant, thinly sliced crosswise

MOTE DE QUESO DE LA NIÑA LOLA

CREAMY YAM SOUP WITH CHEESE

Ñame, or white yam, is a large brown knobby root that can be found in the produce section of Latin American and Asian markets across America. But the key ingredient to this creamy soup, as with many one-pot Colombian meals, is the sautéed onion and scallion base we call *guiso*.

There is an ongoing debate in Colombia about one ingredient that allegedly gives *mote* its true flavor. This is a shrub called *bleo de chupa,* found exclusively in the Sinú River Valley and impossible to find outside the region. Even so, I make *mote* in Brooklyn and serve it with eggplant slices, caramelized onions, and a dash of sriracha.

Prepare the *guiso:* Heat the oil in a Dutch oven or soup pot. Add the onion, and cook over medium-high heat, stirring often, until slightly softened, about 3 minutes. Add the garlic and stir a few times, until fragrant, 30 to 45 seconds. Lower the heat to medium-low and cook until the onion is softened and translucent. Nestle the *ñame* cubes in the onions and cover with cold water. Season with the salt and bring to a simmer. Cook, stirring now and again, until the *ñame* is almost entirely dissolved, 55 minutes to 1 hour. The result will be a creamy, white, thick *mote* soup with a few chunks. Add ¾ pound of the cheese, and cook, stirring, for 3 to 5 minutes, until the cheese starts to melt. You want some whole pieces of cheese left. Turn off the heat, cover, and keep warm.

Meanwhile, prepare the caramelized onions and eggplant: Heat the olive oil in a large skillet over medium heat. Add the onions and cook, stirring often, until the onions take on a deep amber color, 20 to 25 minutes. Add the eggplant slices and continue cooking until the eggplant softens but keeps its shape, 8 to 10 minutes. Set aside.

Right before serving, turn the heat back on to warm up the soup. Add a little water if it is too thick and heat through. Ladle the *mote* into bowls, top with the eggplant, caramelized onions, and remaining ¼ pound cheese, and serve with the *suero* on the side.

Dessert

SERVES 14 TO 16

For the cake

1 cup canned chickpeas, drained, rinsed, and mashed

½ cup pitted prunes, soaked in warm water for 15 minutes

1 tablespoon molasses

¾ cup vegetable oil, divided

1¾ cups whole wheat flour

¾ teaspoon baking powder

½ teaspoon baking soda

Kosher salt

2 large organic eggs

2 tablespoons tahini

1 tablespoon vanilla extract

2 cups brown sugar

For the filling

1 pint frozen plain Greek yogurt or vanilla ice cream

2 tablespoons lime zest

Juice of 1 lime

2 pints mango sorbet

For the meringue

6 egg whites, at room temperature

½ teaspoon cream of tartar

1 cup superfine sugar

1 tablespoon pure vanilla extract

ALASKA DE MANGO Y AJONJOLÍ

MANGO-SESAME BAKED ALASKA

In the previous century, my great-grandfather Don Félix Turbay left Beirut in search of new beginnings oceans away. He found an opportunity in one of the smallest of Colombia's towns, Sincelejo, about thirty miles inland from the Caribbean coast. Don Félix, with his wife, Neyla, started a textile shop near the town's only square. Along with other Lebanese families, the community was anchored and soon enough there were fields of sesame and eggplant growing in backyards to keep the Mediterranean cuisine tradition alive.

In this sleepy town, one of the few attractions was the Heladería Alaska, the only ice cream shop in the town square. As kids we would look forward to going there and tasting all the unusual ice cream flavors: corn, *ñame*, yuca, pumpkin, *guandú* (pigeon pea), sesame. Cuisine experimentation brewed as a result of resourcefulness and community. I loved it, so much so that I created a baked Alaska in honor of this ice cream shop's name.

I have to admit this dessert is not a Colombian tradition. But the Alaska ice cream shop in Sincelejo deserves a loving tribute.

Preheat the oven to 350°F.

Oil two 9-inch round cake pans and line with parchment paper.

Place the chickpeas, soaked prunes, molasses, and ¼ cup of the vegetable oil in the bowl of a food processor. Pulse until a homogenous, dark paste forms. Reserve.

In a separate small bowl, whisk the flour, baking powder, baking soda, and salt to combine. Reserve.

In a large bowl, whisk together the eggs, the remaining ½ cup vegetable oil, the tahini, vanilla, and brown sugar. With a rubber spatula, fold in half of the prune/molasses mixture then half of the flour mixture, alternating until all of the wet and dry mixtures are incorporated. Do not overmix.

Divide the batter between the prepared pans. If you have the mind of a stylist, as I do, weigh the batter so it is evenly distributed into each cake pan, approximately 16 ounces each. Using an offset spatula, spread the batter evenly in the pans. Transfer to the oven and bake until a toothpick comes out clean and the sides of the cake begin to pull away from the sides of the pan, 20 to 25 minutes. Place the cakes on a cooling rack for 10 minutes, then invert onto a plate. Transfer the two cakes back to the rack and cool completely. Cut each cake in half horizontally with a large serrated knife. You should have a total of 4 rounds, each measuring about ¼-inch thick.

Pull the frozen yogurt or ice cream out of the freezer to soften slightly. You want the pint to give when the container is squeezed between your hands, but it should not be fully melted. Working quickly, fold in the lime zest and juice, and return to the freezer for a few minutes.

Line a 10-inch, 20-cup metal bowl with plastic wrap. Place one of the cake rounds on the bottom of the bowl, pressing slightly so that the slice takes on the domed shape. Scoop one-third of the frozen yogurt and evenly spread it atop the base layer of the cake. Cover with plastic wrap and freeze for 20 minutes. Return the remaining yogurt to the freezer.

Remove the dome from the freezer, peel the plastic off the yogurt, add ½ pint of the mango sorbet, and spread it over the frozen yogurt. Cover with the reserved plastic and freeze again for 20 minutes.

Remove the bowl from the freezer, take off the plastic wrap, and top with another cake slice. Press down on the slice and repeat the process with the remaining frozen yogurt, sorbet, and cake rounds, freezing for 20 minutes after each addition of yogurt and sorbet and pressing every time so that the layers adhere well. The top layer should be the final cake round. Cover with plastic wrap and freeze for at least 4 hours after the last addition.

Before serving, remove the bowl from the freezer to temper and make the meringue.

Meringue

Clean a large metal bowl very well—I like using a cloth with a bit of white vinegar. Place the egg whites and cream of tartar in the prepared bowl. Begin whisking slowly, with a handheld or stand mixer, and increase the speed little by little. When the whites begin to become fluffy, slowly add the sugar as you continue mixing on high speed, until the meringue is glossy and holds a nice stiff peak. Add the vanilla extract toward the end.

Assemble

Take the dome out of the freezer, remove the plastic wrap, and invert it onto a rimmed platter. Knock it a few times and you'll hear the thump when it detaches from the bowl. Lift the bowl and peel off the plastic wrap. Spread the meringue over the dome, making swirls all around with your spatula—have fun! Shake your shoulders a bit and reward yourself with a lick from the spatula.

Browning the meringue

Blowtorch method: Using a pastry blowtorch, brown the meringue as dark or as light as you like—personally, I find that there is a bit more drama with the darker browning—it will also photograph better.

Oven method: Place an oven rack close to the source of heat, but with enough room for you to be able to watch the browning process. Turn the broiler to high, place the Alaska dome under the range, and rotate as you begin to smell the toasty meringue.

Slice into thin wedges and serve with a glass of aged rum or a strong espresso to seal the deal.

ARUSÍ PACÍFICO

Located where the lush, dense jungle meets the ocean, Colombia's Pacific coastal region is called El Chocó. Considered one of the wettest places in the world due to its high rainfall, this vast, biodiverse locale is inhabited almost exclusively by Afro-Colombian and indigenous populations.

I first visited El Chocó when I was about sixteen years old. I stayed in Gorgona, an island thirty-five kilometers off the coast. The island is known for a prison that once operated there, and although it closed in 1984, the ruins still stand. The area is also known for its wildlife, including poisonous snakes, migrant whales, and monkeys. I was visiting along with forty other teenage girls as part of a school trip. Everywhere we went, the monkeys would sneak up on us, stealing our clothes and food. The beach was filled with hermit crabs and the sun seldom came out. Needless to say, such a place made an impression on the squeamish city girl that I was.

This school trip marked my sole visit to El Chocó . . . right up until just a few weeks before I finished writing this book. Oh, am I delighted to say that my brother Camilo worked his mastery and in a day planned a trip to the jungle! So there I flew, twenty years later, in a tiny plane, too small for my nerves. We landed in Nuquí, a town on the northern side of the coast. From there, we took a two-hour boat ride southbound along the entire Tribugá Gulf, with the mountainous jungles on our left, all the way to Aursí, a tiny village of only five hundred people. Nature's grandeur humbled me with every passing minute.

Naturally, I quickly made my way into the kitchen of the house that hosted us. I needed to understand what the food would be like in this thick rain forest, next to the ocean, cooked in the powerful brew of long-held traditions and beliefs. The kitchen was an open space, perched on a cliff three hundred feet up, overlooking the water. There were large bundles of plantains hanging from the ceiling, a few bubbling pots of rice, sacks of yuca that would last weeks, and a vat of freshly caught fish. And there she was. Marinela standing in front of the pots, evidently in charge. She wasn't really having my curiosity when I first approached her. But I went back into the kitchen after dinner and thanked her for a most delicious *encocado*, a fish stew slowly cooked in coconut milk accompanied by her addictive, crispy *papa china* (taro root). Still, no response. After a few more meals and a few sips of the locally distilled drink named *biche*, I mustered up the courage to walk into the kitchen for a third time and finally broke the ice by asking: "Marinela, what do you love to eat?" She laughed, and our food talk began.

I write this menu as a way to honor Marinela, her community, and their knowledge. A set of skills that spans unexpected ingredients from game meats, both wild and domestic, to shellfish and every use one can possibly give to the coconut. A treasure chest of knowledge for cooks worldwide.

Cocktail

APERITIVO BAR (see "How I Host," below)
REFRESCO DE PANELA Y GENGIBRE AHUMADO A LA BELLIN
Bellin's Smoky Panela & Ginger Spritzer

Starters

PATACÓNES CON HOGAO Crispy Plantains with Tomato Onion Stew
ENCOCADO DE PIANGUAS DE GUAPI Minty Clam Soup with Plantains & Potatoes

Main

ARROZ ATOLLADO DE PATO
Sticky Duck Rice with Sausage & Eggs

Dessert

POSTRE DE COCO RALLADO & HOJAS DE LIMÓN
Candied Coconut & Kaffir Lime

SETTING THE SCENE

I like to evoke the jungle of the Gulf of Tribugá with simple branches and tropical leaves, dark earthenware, vessels of different shapes, woven runners, and layered placemats. Dark linen napkins, wooden serving utensils, and rustic platters round out the mood.

HOW I HOST

A charming bar with different choices of *aperitivos* and liqueurs, from Lillet (a favorite of ours, served on ice with an orange slice, see page 92) to Campari and from rum to aguardiente. This is perfect for guests to mix their own drink and give you more time to enjoy yourself. These liqueurs can be easily made into a spritz with the addition of sparkling wine, ginger beer, or club soda.

SETTING UP AN
APERITIVO BAR
CHECKLIST

LIQUEURS AND APERITIVOS	☐ Rum La Hechicera ☐ White vermouth ☐ Sherry La Gitana ☐ Sparkling wine (Cui Cui Cremant d'Alsace, Prosecco, or La Jara Prosecco Frizzante)	☐ Aguardiente Antioqueño ☐ Lillet Blanc ☐ Aperol ☐ Campari
MIXERS	☐ Club soda ☐ Patillazo (page 218) ☐ Colombiana Soda	☐ Ginger beer, Belvoir Ginger Beer Presse ☐ Pineapple juice (page 68)
GARNISHES	☐ Lemon slices ☐ Orange slices	☐ Cherries, fresh or Luxardo maraschino
TOOLS	☐ 1- and 2-ounce jigger cups ☐ Napkins ☐ Ice bucket with tongs	☐ Wineglasses or rocks glasses (make your life easier by using only one or two types of glasses) ☐ Large beverage tub filled with ice
BITS AND BITES	☐ *Patacónes con Hogao* (page 171) ☐ *Pan de Arroz* (page 206)	☐ Chicharrónes (packaged pork rinds) ☐ Pandebonos (page 110)
COCKTAILS AND MIXES	☐ Rum La Hechicera + ginger beer + ice + lemon slice ☐ Aperol + Prosecco + club soda + orange slice ☐ Campari + Patillazo + soda ☐ Aguardiente Antioqueño + ice + lime slice	☐ Lillet Blanc + Crémant + cherry ☐ Sherry La Gitana, straight up ☐ Smoky Panela (page 170) + ginger spritzer

PLAYLIST

The country's Afro-Colombian roots still grow along the Pacific Ocean. The food, the beats, and the culture, mixed with some catchy tunes.

"La Victoria" by Chancha Vía Circuito (featuring Lido Pimienta & Manu Ranks)
"Bonfo" by Fela Kuti & His Koola Lobitos
"Banana Boat" by Michiko Hamamura
"Old Devil Moon" by Chet Baker
"Te Invito" by Herencia de Timbiqui
"Sabrosura" by Sebastián Yatra, Piso 2, Herencia de Timbique & Martina La Peligrosa
"Somos Pacifico" by ChoQuibTown
"River" by Ibeyi
"Muévelo" by Salt Cathedral
"Somos Dos" by Bomba Estéreo

Cocktail

MAKES 8 SERVINGS

¼ cup ground panela

One 2-inch piece fresh ginger, peeled, sliced into rounds

2 cups boiling water

2 bags lapsang souchong tea or any other smoked tea

4 cups ice cold water

½ cup fresh lime juice

Ice

16 cups club soda

REFRESCO DE PANELA Y GENGIBRE AHUMADO Á BELLIN

BELLIN'S SMOKY PANELA & GINGER SPRITZER

Evoking the woody scent and imparted taste of wood-fire cooking, this refreshing, smoky drink gets its deep flavors both from the panela and the tea. The sparkling club soda and sour lime make this the perfect non-alcoholic option for the aperitivo bar.

Since I cannot bring the regional style of outdoor cooking to this menu, I can at least bring the sensation of gathering around a wood-fire stove. The name Bellin is in honor of the owner of the beautiful garden where we photographed these scenes.

Place the *panela* and ginger slices in a small saucepan. Cover with the boiling water and cook over medium-high heat, stirring now and then, until the panela dissolves. Turn off the heat and add the tea bags. Cover and steep for 8 to 10 minutes. Strain, discard the tea bags and ginger, and refrigerate the tea until chilled. Before serving, combine the sweetened ginger tea with the cold water and lime juice in a large pitcher. Serve over ice in highball glasses topped with the club soda.

For the hogao

1 tablespoon canola oil

2 large yellow onions, finely diced

6 scallions, white and green parts, chopped

4 ripe plum tomatoes, grated or finely chopped

4 orange bell peppers, seeded, deveined, and finely chopped

4 garlic cloves, grated

2 tablespoons white wine vinegar

1 teaspoon ground cumin

1 teaspoon ground achiote

Kosher salt and freshly ground black pepper

For the *patacónes*

Canola oil

4 large green plantains, peeled, cut into 1-inch rounds

4 large garlic cloves, peeled

Sea salt

PATACONES CON HOGAO

CRISPY PLANTAINS WITH TOMATO & ONION STEW

This is the Colombian iteration of chips and guacamole, except there are no corn chips or avocados. Instead of chips, there is a fried plantain disc—crispy on the outside, fluffy on the inside—known as the *patacón*.

The *hogao*, on the other hand, has many names: the Spaniards call it *sofrito*, some Central American islands know it as creole sauce, and we Colombians tend to call it *guiso*, depending on the ingredients. It's traditionally made with scallions and tomatoes, but it can also include yellow onions, garlic, cumin, salt, and pepper, all sautéed over low heat. Instead of being used as a dip, the *hogao* is usually scooped up and topped on each *patacón* for generous bites.

Make the *patacónes*

Pour 2 inches of oil into a medium Dutch oven or other heavy pot. Attach a deep-fry thermometer and bring the temperature to 350°F over medium-high heat. Meanwhile, line a sheet tray or platter with paper towels.

Using a spider or slotted spoon, submerge 3 or 4 pieces of the plantains at a time into the preheated oil. Fry, shifting the plantains from side to side to maintain the heat and cook evenly, until softened and light golden brown, 6 to 8 minutes. Lift from the oil onto the lined sheet tray and carefully, while still hot, press down to flatten using an oiled tortilla maker, a small skillet, or a river stone. Repeat with the remaining plantain pieces. Once all the plantains have been pressed and are cool enough to handle, rub the plantains with the garlic, and lay down fresh draining paper towels. Reheat the same oil to 375°F, and refry the *patacónes* in batches, 4 or 5 at a time, while moving them around with the spider, until crispy and light golden brown, 4 to 5 minutes. Remove from the oil, drain, sprinkle with salt, and serve.

To make the *hogao*

Heat the oil in a large skillet. Add the onions and scallions and cook, stirring often, until the onions soften, 3 to 4 minutes. Add the tomatoes, bell peppers, garlic, vinegar, cumin, and achiote and cook over low heat, stirring occasionally, until the vegetables soften and the juices thicken slightly, 18 to 20 minutes. Remove from the heat and season with salt and pepper to taste.

**SERVES 8 AS AN APPETIZER;
4 TO 6 AS A MAIN COURSE**

36 cockles or littleneck
clams, scrubbed

2 tablespoons cornmeal

2 cups Refrito Verde
(recipe follows)

½ cup aguardiente or Pernod

2 green plantains, peeled
and cut into small chunks
with a teaspoon

½ pound new potatoes,
scrubbed

4 cups clam juice
or 2 cups water

1 (13.5-ounce) can
coconut milk

Kosher salt and freshly
ground black pepper

¼ cup chopped spearmint,
plus more for garnish

White Rice (page 113)

3 limes, cut into wedges

For the Refrito Verde
MAKES 2 CUPS

2 tablespoons extra-virgin
olive oil

2 yellow onions, finely
chopped (2¼ cups)

4 garlic cloves,
minced or grated

4 scallions, white and green
parts, chopped (½ cup)

2 Italian green peppers,
Cubanelle peppers, or
Anaheim chilis, seeded,
deveined, and chopped

1 green Thai chili or
ají chili, chopped

Kosher salt and freshly
ground black pepper

1 cup chopped cilantro,
both leaves and stems

10 ounces spinach,
very finely chopped

ENCOCADO DE PIANGUAS DE GUAPI

MINTY COCKLE OR CLAM SOUP WITH PLANTAINS & POTATOES

Pianguas are freshwater black and white cockles that live in the muddy mangrove banks off the town of Guapi on the Pacific coast. These cherry-size mollusks are one of the pillars of the town's local cuisine, and their sharp shells are used as a cooking tool. An old recipe I found in the archives of the National Library's collection of traditional cooking instructed cooks to "grate two green plantains using *piangua* shells."

Since *pianguas* rarely make it out of the town of Guapi, littleneck clams or cockles are a perfect substitute and make a quick weeknight dinner. Submerging the clams in a bowl of cold water with a dash of cornmeal helps cleanse the mollusks of sand and other impurities.

Making a double or triple batch of *refrito* to keep in the fridge is a shortcut to a faster meal any day.

Place the clams in a large bowl, cover with fresh cold water, and sprinkle in the cornmeal. Leave for 20 to 40 minutes to give the clams a chance to filter out the sand and release impurities. Remove each clam from the water and scrub.

Meanwhile, prepare the Refrito Verde: Pour the oil into a large pot (large enough to hold the clams) and heat over medium-high heat. Add the onions and garlic and cook, stirring now and then, until fragrant, 45 to 50 seconds. Stir in the scallions, green peppers, and chili, and season with salt and pepper to taste. Continue cooking over low heat until the vegetables soften, about 10 minutes. Add the cilantro and spinach and stir to combine. Cook until the spinach wilts, 2 to 3 minutes. Pour in the *aguardiente* while scraping the brown bits from the bottom of the pot with a spatula and cook until the alcohol evaporates, about 1 minute. Add the plantains, potatoes, clam juice, and coconut milk and season with salt and pepper to taste. Once the liquid comes to a boil, raise the heat to medium-low and cook until the potatoes and plantains are tender, 10 to 12 minutes.

Add the clams and spearmint. Stir to combine and nestle the clams into the broth. Cover and cook until the clams open, 8 to 10 minutes.

Place 4 or 5 clams into each serving bowl (discard any that don't open) and ladle the broth and veggies over. Set out a fork and spoon for each guest. Serve with a side of white rice and the lime wedges.

ARROZ ATOLLADO DE PATO

STICKY DUCK RICE WITH SAUSAGE & EGGS

SERVES 8 TO 10

6 whole duck legs
(3½ pounds), leg and thigh
separated, excess fat trimmed

1 tablespoon kosher salt

2 teaspoons freshly ground
black pepper

2 teaspoons ground allspice

2 garlic cloves, grated

4 medium (1½ pounds)
spicy Italian sausages,
cut into ½-inch slices on
the bias

2 medium yellow onions,
diced (2 cups)

4 large scallions,
white and green parts,
chopped (¾ cup)

1 tablespoon tomato paste

2 tablespoons sriracha
(optional)

2 teaspoons ground achiote

2 teaspoons grated fresh
turmeric root, or 1 teaspoon
ground turmeric

1 teaspoon ground cumin

1 (14.5-ounce) can diced
tomatoes, drained

2 green bell peppers, seeded,
deveined, and diced

2 long cilantro stems,
plus 1½ cups fresh
cilantro leaves

2¼ cups long-grain
white rice

10 cups water

4 large organic hard-boiled
eggs, peeled and quartered,
or 10 hard-boiled quail eggs,
peeled and left whole

Game birds are not the first thing that springs to mind when it comes to the food of the tropics; however, they are quite abundant in the wetlands of el Chocó, and ancestral techniques for slow-cooking fowl over coals and leaves have kept these recipes alive. The name *atollado* comes from *toyo*, a type of small shark that used to be smoked and dried in the town of Guapi. One of the recipes for rice was a stewy porridge using the smoked shark meat. The term *atollado* is now used to describe the soupy consistency of the dish—thankfully, it no longer needs to include shark meat.

This rice can also be marvelous made with chicken. Simply add 2 tablespoons canola oil in the searing step.

This dish is great for feeding a crowd with a leafy salad alongside.

Rinse and pat dry the duck legs. In a small bowl, combine the salt, pepper, allspice, and garlic. Rub the duck legs all over with the spice mixture. Cover with plastic wrap and refrigerate for at least 2 hours or, if you have time, overnight.

Heat a large cast-iron or Dutch oven over high heat and sear the marinated duck legs in two batches until golden, 2 to 3 minutes per side. You will see there is enough fat in the skin so there is no need for added oil. Turn off the heat and remove the duck legs from the pot.

Carefully remove all but 2 tablespoons of the rendered duck fat and keep it for roasting potatoes. Reheat the pot over medium-high heat, and add the sausages, cooking until light golden brown, about 2 minutes on each side. Add the onions and scallions and stir, scraping the bottom of the pot with the back of a wooden spoon. Cook until the onions soften and become slightly translucent, about 4 minutes. Add the tomato paste, sriracha, if using, the achiote, turmeric, cumin, tomatoes, bell peppers, and cilantro stems and stir to combine. Season with a pinch of salt. Add the rice, and swirl the grains around so that they are coated with the tomato-vegetable mixture. Return the seared duck to the pot, arranging the pieces in a single layer. Cover with the water and bring to a boil. Lower the heat to medium-low and simmer until the rice begins to soften, 20 to 25 minutes. Reduce the heat to very low, cover, and cook until the rice puffs and some liquid remains, 15 to 18 minutes. Transfer the rice to a platter, and garnish with the hard-boiled eggs and cilantro leaves.

Dessert

SERVES 6 TO 8

6 cups grated fresh coconut (3 medium coconuts; see page 75), or frozen grated coconut, thawed

1 cup sugar

7 ounces kaffir lime leaves or orange leaves (optional)

2 cinnamon sticks

¼ cup rice flour

Zest of 3 limes

POSTRE DE COCO RALLADO & HOJAS DE LIMA

CANDIED COCONUT & KAFFIR LIME

Desserts from this region are typically infused with orange leaves to impart a fragrant citrus and floral scent. A good replacement is kaffir lime leaves, which have a bright fresh taste—these can be found frozen at Thai markets. I love a light and easy dessert that keeps well. This one is an especially good one because it has no dairy and will last in the refrigerator, covered, for up to a week. I suggest serving in small bowls or glasses with a dessert fork.

Place the grated coconut and sugar in a large pot and cover with water. Bring to a boil and cook over medium heat, stirring now and then, until the sugar dissolves and the liquid starts to thicken, about 30 minutes.

Lower the heat, add the kaffir lime leaves, rice flour, and cinnamon sticks and continue cooking until the coconut has absorbed most of the water. Stir in the lime zest, remove the cinnamon sticks and kaffir leaves, and carefully transfer the coconut mixture to a serving dish or glass container.

Place in the refrigerator and chill for at least 1 hour. To serve, scoop into individual small bowls.

EMPANADA SATURNALIA

Empanada Saturnalia is the name I give to a feast where everyone gets involved. From Argentina to the Philippines to Ecuador to Colombia, the empanada is one and the same. The word means to "enbread"— literally to wrap or coat in bread. As simple as it is, we all give it different fillings, and with that, distinct souls and stories. So, get creative and invite friends over to cook, drink, and make empanadas (not necessarily in that order). I like to serve rosé, one or two shots of *aguardiente,* or mezcal on ice.

Guests can roll, fill, and fold the empanadas to either cook and eat right away, or to take home and stock up their freezers (they keep well frozen for three months). It's even easier if everyone brings their own to-go containers.

Although it might not seem like it, making empanadas is a simple process. First you prepare your fillings, then you work on the doughs, assemble the empanadas, and finally you either fry or bake them. That's it! For these, I use a recipe with both wheat flour and corn; for a traditional cornmeal recipe, see *Empanaditas de Pipián* (page 108)—which is perfect for baking.

Make a large batch of Ají (page 145) and cut limes into small wedges. Either make the fillings in advance for your guests to assemble or start from scratch once everyone arrives.

Empanada Fillings

ROASTED CHICKEN & CORIANDER

**MAKES 1½ CUPS
(24 TABLESPOONS)**

2 tablespoons extra-virgin olive oil

1 medium yellow onion, finely chopped

1 medium red bell pepper, seeded, deveined, and finely chopped

¼ teaspoon kosher salt

Freshly ground black pepper

2 teaspoons coriander seeds, toasted and ground

1 teaspoon ground cumin

½ teaspoon ground turmeric

1¾ cups finely chopped roasted chicken, white and dark meat

5 tablespoons sour cream

¼ cup finely chopped fresh cilantro leaves and stems

All fillings make enough for 16 to 20 large snack-size empanadas, using 4-inch discs, or 32 to 36 smaller cocktail-size empanadas using a 3-inch disc. Dough recipes and assembly instructions follow.

In a medium skillet, heat the oil over medium heat. Cook the onion and pepper until lightly browned, 3 to 5 minutes. Add the salt, pepper to taste, the coriander, cumin, and turmeric, and stir well with a wooden spoon. Cook for 1 minute.

Lower the heat to medium-low and add the chicken to the skillet. Stir well, making sure you scrape all bits and pieces stuck to the skillet. Transfer the chicken mixture to a medium bowl and let cool.

Add the sour cream and cilantro to the cooled chicken and mix well with a fork. The filling should be moist but not too wet, for perfect empanadas. Set aside until you are ready to stuff your empanadas.

GROUND BEEF & YUKON GOLD POTATOES

**MAKES 1½ CUPS
(24 TABLESPOONS)**

Kosher salt

6 medium Yukon Gold potatoes, peeled and quartered

10 ounces ground beef

2 garlic cloves, finely minced or grated

2 tablespoon unsalted butter, divided

1 small onion, grated

1 whole tomato, grated

Freshly ground black pepper

1 egg, beaten (if baking the empanadas)

Ají, for serving (page 145)

In a small saucepan, bring 2 to 3 cups of water to a boil and add 1 teaspoon salt. Add the potatoes, and boil for 8 to 10 minutes, until soft. Make sure you don't overboil the potatoes, as they cook fast and will easily fall apart.

Meanwhile, mix the beef, garlic, and a pinch of salt in a small bowl using your hands. Reserve.

Drain the potatoes into a colander. Place the hot potatoes back into the saucepan and, using a fork, mash with 1 tablespoon of the butter. Let the mashed potatoes cool. Reserve.

Heat the remaining 1 tablespoon butter in a medium skillet over medium-high heat. Add the onion, tomato, and salt to taste, and cook for 3 to 5 minutes, stirring with a wooden spoon. Add the reserved ground beef mixture and break it up with the wooden spoon. Cook until the beef is cooked through, 2 to 3 minutes. Season with a touch of salt and pepper to taste.

Turn the heat off and add the mashed potatoes into the skillet. Mix until the meat and potatoes are well combined. Reserve until the mixture has cooled completely and you are ready to stuff your empanadas.

**MAKES 1½ CUPS
(24 TABLESPOONS)**

1 whole pineapple, peeled, cored, and cut into ¼-inch dice (4 cups)

½ cup water

½ cup sugar

2 cinnamon sticks

4 cardamom pods, crushed

6 whole cloves

6 whole allspice berries

Kosher salt

8 ounces goat cheese (or cream cheese), at room temperature

1 teaspoon honey

2 tablespoons finely minced fresh thyme, or 2 tablespoons finely minced fresh rosemary

Kosher salt and freshly ground black pepper

DULCE DE PIÑA

CANDIED PINEAPPLE WITH WHIPPED GOAT CHEESE

In a medium saucepan over medium-high heat, combine the pineapple, water, sugar, cinnamon sticks, cardamom, cloves, allspice, and a pinch of salt. Cook until the mixture starts to boil. Lower the heat to medium and simmer for 35 to 40 minutes, until most of the liquid is evaporated and the *dulce de piña* is thick. Remove the pan from the heat and let the mixture cool. Remove the spices with a slotted spoon and discard.

Reserve until you are ready to make empanadas.

For the whipped goat cheese: In the bowl of a stand mixer fitted with the whisk attachment, whip the goat cheese on medium speed until light and fluffy, about 5 minutes.

Add the honey and thyme to the whipped cheese, season with salt and pepper to taste, and mix until fully incorporated.

Transfer to a small bowl and set aside until you are ready to stuff your empanadas.

Empanada Doughs

MAKES 30 TO 32 EMPANADAS
(3-INCH DIAMETER, COCKTAIL
SIZE) OR 16 EMPANADAS
(4-INCH DIAMETER, SNACK
SIZE)

1½ cups (12 ounces) all-purpose flour, plus more for dusting

½ cup (4 ounces) fine corn flour

1 teaspoon kosher salt

6 tablespoons (3 ounces) unsalted butter, melted

7 ounces plain unsweetened Greek yogurt

2 to 3 tablespoons warm water or milk (or more depending on atmospheric humidity)

DOUGH FOR SAVORY FILLINGS

In a large bowl, whisk together the all-purpose flour, corn flour, and salt. Add the melted butter and incorporate with a fork. Add the yogurt and mix again. At this point you will have flour that has not been incorporated into the wet ingredients. Add the water, 1 tablespoon at a time, and, using your hands, incorporate the water until a smooth ball forms.

Divide the dough into two pieces. Reserve one piece in a bowl covered with a damp, clean kitchen towel so it doesn't dry out. Line two or three baking sheets with parchment paper, depending on the size of empanadas you choose to make.

With one piece at a time, on a floured surface, roll out the dough with a rolling pin, pressing from the center out until it reaches a ⅛- to ¼-inch thickness. Using a round cookie cutter, 3- or 4-inch diameter, press down on the dough, making sure the cutter goes all the way through. Make sure to cut the discs very close to one another to make the best use of the dough.

Place the discs on the prepared baking sheet and cover with the damp kitchen towel you used to cover the dough.

Form a ball with the leftover pieces of dough and roll out again. Repeat the same steps for cutting out the dough.

Note: The second time you roll out the dough, you will notice that it is rubbery and a little harder to work with. (Also, when you cut it out, you will notice the discs will spring back a bit and will be a bit smaller than in the first round.)

You should have 30 to 32 discs if you used a 3-inch cutter, or 16 discs if you used a 4-inch cutter.

At this point, you can fill the empanadas with a savory filling: Roasted Chicken & Coriander (page 180) or Ground Beef & Yukon Gold Potatoes (page 180). Instructions for assembling follow on page 186.

A LA MESA

**MAKES 16 EMPANADAS
(4-INCH DIAMETER,
SNACK SIZE) OR 25
BITE-SIZE EMPANADAS
(3-INCH DIAMETER)**

3 cups (15 ounces)
all-purpose flour, plus more
for dusting

½ teaspoon kosher salt

1 teaspoon baking powder

8 tablespoons (4 ounces)
unsalted butter, melted

Zest of 1 orange

¼ cup orange juice

⅔ cup club soda

DOUGH FOR SWEET FILLINGS

Mix the flour, salt, and baking powder in the bowl of a food processor, and pulse until well combined. Add the butter and pulse until combined and sandy, about 15 seconds.

Add the orange zest and juice and pulse until combined, about 15 seconds.

Add the club soda (in small increments) and continue pulsing until a clumpy dough forms.

Remove the dough from the food processor and place on a well-floured surface. Form a smooth ball and divide the dough in half. Line a baking sheet with parchment paper and set aside.

Roll out half of the dough with a rolling pin, pressing from the center out until it is ¼ inch thick. Using a round cookie cutter, 3- or 4-inch diameter, press down on the dough, making sure the cutter goes all the way through. Make sure to cut the discs very close to one another to make the best use of the dough.

Place the discs on a baking sheet lined with parchment paper and cover with a damp kitchen towel. Repeat the process with the rest of the dough.

You should have 25 to 28 discs if you used a 3-inch cutter, or 16 discs if you used a 4-inch cutter.

At this point, you can fill the empanadas with a sweet filling: Dulce de Piña (page 182). Instructions for assembling follow.

Empanadas . . . Assemble!

Use 1 to 1½ teaspoons of filling for 3-inch round empanadas and 1 to 1½ tablespoons for 4-inch empanadas.

Make sure that you don't underfill (the empanada will be too doughy) or overfill (the filling will leak out).

To seal the empanadas, fold the dough over the filling (you will now have a half-moon shape) and seal the edges by pressing the dough with your fingers. If you're having a hard time sealing the edges, you can brush the inside edges with egg (1 egg, beaten)—it will act as a glue for the empanadas. You can also use a fork to help seal the edges; just press the tines against the edges.

If cooking right away, transfer the empanadas to the freezer for at least 30 minutes. The empanadas can be stored in the freezer for up to 3 months wrapped in plastic, and don't need thawing before baking or frying. Simply add 10 to 12 minutes to the cooking time.

At this point, you can either bake or fry your empanadas.

Empanada Cooking

For baking

Preheat the oven to 375°F for smaller empanadas and 400°F for larger ones.

If you want your empanadas to have a nice golden finish, brush them with an egg wash (1 egg whisked with a few drops of water).

Bake until golden, 18 to 25 minutes.

4 cups canola oil

For frying

Heat the oil to 350°F in the heavy-bottomed pot of a *caldero*, using a deep-fry thermometer. Line a large platter with paper towels and set aside. The oil should bubble when you add the empanadas. Fry in small batches until they are golden brown on each side. Don't overcrowd the pot, and if any of the empanadas break and leak, immediately remove them from the oil.

Place the fried empanadas on the prepared platter to drain any excess oil.

La Nena Sierra

La Nena is a nickname that roughly translates to "the babe." It's also a term of endearment in Colombian Spanish. This babe was born in Bogotá, Colombia's capital city, where she studied tourism and travel administration. Just like her friend Vivi, La Nena is an entrepreneur who spent seven years building her own hospitality business in Colombia, until she eventually fell in love with video and film, which took her to New York City. La Nena studied film production at NYU and produced several TV commercials, films, and soap operas during her early years in the city. Yet, her dormant passion for food and hospitality was always present and boiled over about a decade ago when she decided to open a Colombian arepa truck called Palenque.

She has grown this business over the years and now proudly owns a brick-and-mortar restaurant where she does it all: management, sales, marketing, and social media. In other words, she is still a producer. La Nena makes great arepas happen: healthy, hearty, and always on time.

EL ALGO

This time of day has many names in Spanish: *el algo, las onces, entre-día, tente en pie*. Their direct translation to English is confusing to say the least: "the something," "the elevens," "hold you up." Still, these phrases all refer to the simplest concept: the snack.

These are the craved foods we allow ourselves in between meals. The word "snack" is actually descriptive not only of the size of this dish but its practicality as well. A reason to pause and recharge, an excuse to gather and/or squeeze in a little extra time with friends during the workday.

Hosting in-between meals scratches my baking itch. Sweet and savory toasts with *panela* and a glass of red as an early evening *aperitivo* or crispy rice bread rings with a hot cup of coffee as an afternoon pick-me-up or *tente en pie*.

Refreshing and soothing drinks are a doorway to unexpected pairings: the chunky drink *champús* (made of diced pineapple and corn with crushed ice, page 221) provides relief on any hot summer day, and the *panela* ginger infusion (page 222) promises to comfort and energize. The guava and feta *pastelitos* (page 210) served with hot tea or a glass of sherry help to warm up late fall afternoons.

Traditional recipes also fill this chapter with delicious comforts, from the iconic *mogollas* (page 198), a small sweet and savory bun sold in neighborhood bakeries all over Colombia, to *cucas* (page 202), the chewy spiced molasses cookies sold everywhere from stoplights to bodegas. The majority of these are eaten between breakfast and lunch, at around 11 a.m. Hence the meaning behind *las onces*, or the elevens. But they are also true *pasteles*, as cookies and drinks are also an afternoon ritual.

All of these delicious foods are available all year long. Just like Bogotá's rainy days.

SERVES 4

4 slices sourdough Pullman loaf, ½ to ¼ inch thick

1½ tablespoons salted butter, cut into 4 cubes, softened

¼ cup grated panela

Flaky sea salt

2 ounces Serrano ham slices (optional)

TOSTADAS CON PANELA

TOAST WITH BUTTER AND PANELA

In spite of the elaborate dishes one can find in the long list of pastries, breads, and cookies of Colombian afternoon treats, I chose to include these toasts with panela, which are totally made up by my family—they don't even earn the recipe qualification because they are simple yet decadent and surprisingly easy.

You can glam these up as a cocktail bite with the addition of a few slices of Serrano ham, draped over the bubbling panela. I use a yeasty sourdough Pullman loaf and flaky sea salt to add a layer of flavor and texture.

Preheat the broiler to low.

Place the bread slices on a baking sheet and broil until they toast to a pale brown, 3 to 4 minutes, watching them closely to make sure they don't burn. Remove from the oven and spread each piece of toast with 1 cube butter and sprinkle with 1 tablespoon *panela*. Return to the broiler and broil until the panela starts to melt and bubble, 2 to 3 minutes. Sprinkle with sea salt to taste and drape a slice of Serrano ham over each piece of bread, if using. Serve cut in half crosswise.

MAKES 24 SMALL BUNS

For the dough

3½ tablespoons melted butter, plus 1½ tablespoons butter to grease the bowl and mold and 1 tablespoon to brush the buns

¼ cup warm water

1 package quick-acting dry yeast

¼ cup plus 1 teaspoon granulated sugar

3 ¼ cups all-purpose flour, plus more for dusting

½ cup wheat germ

1 teaspoon kosher salt

2 teaspoons ground coriander

¾ cup plus 2 tablespoons warm whole milk, plus more if needed

For the *chicharrón* filling

8 tablespoons unsalted butter, melted and divided

2½ ounces packaged unsalted pork rinds (about 2½ cups, depending on how they are cut)

¼ cup grated panela or packed dark brown sugar

2 teaspoons coriander seeds, toasted and ground with a mortar and pestle

Zest from 2 large oranges (2 tablespoons)

1 teaspoon flaky sea salt, plus more for garnish

Equipment

9-inch springform pan

Large metal bowl

MOGOLLAS CHICHARRÓNAS

PORK, ORANGE & CORIANDER BUNS

Girardot is a sweltering tropical town that sits on the banks of the Magdalena, the country's largest river: a wide, sandy body of water flowing from jungle to beaches to open plains. Girardot's main square is shaded by acacia trees, the flowers of which filter the light, casting a coral tint over the courtyard. The hot, humid air reminds you that you are almost below sea level. During the day, the town buzzes with motorcycles and bikes.

The town square is surrounded by makeshift dance clubs blasting loud music and boasting amateur DJs, but there are also havens like Panificadora el Sol, a decades-old baking institution that sells everything from dinner rolls to bright pink, blue, and green birthday cakes out of a spinning glass display case. One of their specialties is the *mogolla chicharróna*, a buttery, sweet, and savory wheat-germ pastry filled with pork cracklings and brown sugar.

Small but decadent, the original *mogollas* can be a tad dry. I have taken the liberty to modify the filling by adding orange zest and coriander. Try to find the meatiest pork rinds possible—the ones with not only skin but also a bit of meat attached. (See my favorite brand on page 12).

Dough: Grease a large bowl with the 1½ tablespoons butter; grease an 8-inch cake pan with the 1 tablespoon butter. Set aside.

In a small bowl, mix the warm water with the dry yeast and 1 teaspoon of the sugar. Set aside for 5 minutes or until the yeast activates (the top layer should start to bubble and foam).

In a large bowl, mix the flour, wheat germ, salt, coriander, and remaining ¼ cup sugar. With your fingers, create a deep well in the middle of the flour.

Pour the remaining 3½ tablespoons butter, the milk, and activated yeast into the well. With your fingers, start to incorporate the flour with the liquid until you can form the dough into a ball. If the dough appears dry, add more milk, 1 teaspoon at a time, until it all comes together.

Place the ball on a floured surface and knead for 5 minutes to activate the gluten. Re-form the dough into a soft ball and put it in the reserved greased bowl. Cover with plastic wrap and let the dough rise in a warm place for 2 hours, or until the ball doubles in size.

***Chicharrón* filling:** Combine the pork rinds with 4 tablespoons of the butter, the panela, coriander, zest, and sea salt in a food processor and mix until the ingredients are incorporated and the mixture has the consistency of wet sand. Set aside.

Place the dough on a lightly floured surface and flatten it with your palms to remove air bubbles.

Divide the dough into 24 1½-inch pieces. Flatten each piece into a 3-inch circle and place ½ tablespoon (loosely packed) of the pork rind and coriander filling in the center of each piece of dough. Form into buns by pinching the dough at the seam to keep any filling from spilling out. Arrange the pieces in the prepared cake pan, stacking 2 to 3 layers of small buns. Reserve in a warm place in the kitchen until the buns double in size, 25 to 30 minutes.

Preheat the oven to 350°F.

Before you place the pan in the oven, pour the remaining 4 tablespoons melted butter evenly over the risen buns and sprinkle with the remaining pork rind powder. Bake for 35 to 40 minutes. (I tent the mold with foil at 20 minutes so the buns brown nicely, while the insides are evenly cooked throughout.)

Remove the pan from the oven. Using oven mitts, unclasp the ring and remove. Slide the buns onto a serving plate and serve while they are still hot.

ALEGRÍAS DE COCO Y ANÍS

POPCORN, COCONUT & ANISE JOY BITES

MAKES 16 GOLF-SIZE BALLS

⅓ cup date syrup

3 tablespoons tahini paste

1 cup unsweetened
coconut flakes

2 teaspoons anise seeds

5 cups popcorn
(already popped) or
9 cups popped sorghum

2 to 3 tablespoons vegetable
oil (for coating your hands)

2 to 3 teaspoons flaky
sea salt

"Alegría con coco y anís!" goes the hymn sung by the Palenqueras, women mostly from a small town called San Basilio de Palenque, on the country's northern coast.

Their shouted offering is often heard along the beaches and streets of coastal towns and cities where they walk with large aluminum vats confidently balanced on their heads. The vats hold all sorts of coconut, papaya, pineapple, and *arequipe* sweets, including the coveted *alegrías*. The word *alegrías* is plural in Spanish for joy or happiness. Imagine that: a bowl full of not one but multiple iterations of joy contained within small, bite-size candied fruit.

How can one resist eating a sweet ball of popped sorghum (tiny grains that pop like corn) clumped together with dark caramel, toasted coconut, and a touch of anise seeds? I have made my own version without refined sugar and include tahini paste—a yummy and beneficial fat. You can use regular popcorn or Pipcorn—a brand of mini heirloom corn popped kernels.

Liz Moody, a brilliant cookbook author, wellness writer, and podcaster extraordinaire, asked me, "Why haven't you written a Colombian cookbook yet?" It was her push at the exact time when I needed a push to take the leap that led to this cookbook. Liz, these joy bites are for you.

In a large bowl, stir to combine the date syrup, tahini paste, coconut flakes, and anise seeds. Add the popcorn and incorporate using a large spatula so that the tahini and syrup mixture covers the grains, forming a Rice Krispies-like consistency. Form 16 golf-size balls with well-oiled hands; if the mixture is too sticky, grease your hands with another touch of oil as you go. Sprinkle with the sea salt, and serve.

Alegrías keep for a week stored in a tightly sealed container at room temperature.

**MAKES 28 COOKIES OR
14 COOKIE SANDWICHES**

Spicy Molasses Cookies

1 cup (½ pound) unsalted
butter, at room temperature

¼ cup light brown sugar

¼ cup unsulphured molasses

1 small egg

1¾ cups all-purpose flour

1 teaspoon baking soda

½ teaspoon kosher salt

1 teaspoon ground cinnamon

¼ teaspoon ground cloves

½ teaspoon ground
cardamom

Zest of 1 orange
(about 2 teaspoons)

Malta Ice Cream
(recipe follows)

Equipment

4 baking sheets

2 half sheet pans

Parchment paper

Stand or handheld mixer

Ice cream scoop

CUCAS CON HELADO DE MALTA

SPICY MOLASSES COOKIES WITH MALT ICE CREAM SANDWICHES

Cucas are cakey cookies, similar in texture to whoopie pies, whose name has made generations of mischievous kids chuckle. Along with a Pony Malta they were the ultimate after-school combo: the burnt sugar, spices, and a cakey texture on one side; the bubbly satisfaction of an ice-cold malt soda on the other. These *cucas* are less sweet than regular biscuits, so they are a neutral base for creamy malt ice cream.

Malta is to Colombians what root beer is to Americans. And much like cilantro or Hawaiian pizza, this is quite the divisive taste. You either love or hate it.

But whether you chuckle at the many connotations of the name of the cookies or can't stomach a malty drink, this recipe will make you rethink both. Make the *cucas* in advance and either serve with Malt Ice Cream or your favorite store-bought salted caramel ice cream.

Preheat the oven to 350°F. Line four baking sheets with parchment paper.

In a stand mixer fitted with the paddle attachment, cream the butter and sugar at medium speed until light and fluffy, about 2 minutes. Add the molasses and continue mixing until incorporated. Add the egg and mix until combined, stopping to scrape the sides of the bowl with a rubber spatula.

In a separate bowl, mix together the flour, baking soda, salt, cinnamon, cloves, cardamom, and orange zest. Add the dry ingredients to the creamed butter mixture ½ cup at a time, so that the flour doesn't fly everywhere, and mix until combined.

Using a small ice cream scoop or a tablespoon, scoop the batter onto the baking sheets, placing each scoop about 1 inch apart.

Bake until the cookies are slightly firm—they will still appear soft in the middle but will harden as they cool—12 to 14 minutes, rotating once halfway through baking. Remove from the oven and allow to cool completely.

To assemble the ice cream sandwiches, remove the ice cream from the freezer and let it soften for 3 minutes. Line two half sheet pans with parchment paper.

Place 7 *cucas* bottom side up on one of the pans.

Using an ice cream scoop (regular size), scoop a ball of ice cream and place it in the center of each cookie, working as fast as you can (while being neat) to avoid the ice cream melting.

Continued

With a spoon (or your fingers), flatten the ice cream a bit and place a *cuca* on top to create a sandwich. Repeat the process to finish the other 6 cookie sandwiches.

If the ice cream becomes too soft while assembling, place it back in the freezer for 8 to 10 minutes, remove, and finish the rest of the cookie sandwiches in the second tray. Serve right away or freeze wrapped in waxed freezer paper until ready to eat!

HELADO DE MALTA

Malt Ice Cream

MAKES 6 CUPS (1½ QUARTS)

3 cups malt soda, such as Malta India, or 3 tablespoons malt powder

2 large pasteurized eggs

½ cup sugar

½ cup heavy cream

2 cups whole milk

½ cup powdered milk

½ teaspoon sea salt

Pour the malt soda into a medium saucepan and bring to a boil over high heat. Reduce the heat to low and simmer for 40 minutes or until the liquid is reduced by half. Set aside and let cool completely.

Whisk the eggs and sugar in a bowl with a hand mixer until the mixture becomes pale yellow and ribbony. Pour in the malt reduction or malt powder and whisk well to incorporate. Set aside.

In a separate bowl, whisk the heavy cream, whole milk, powdered milk, and salt until the powdered milk dissolves completely. Pour this mixture into the egg and malt mixture and stir to incorporate.

Refrigerate until very cold, 20 to 30 minutes. Transfer the cold mixture into the pre-chilled bowl of an ice cream machine and churn according to the manufacturer's instructions.

MAKES 50 RINGS

2 cups 2% small-curd cottage cheese

2 cups sweet rice flour

½ cup unsalted butter, chilled and cut into small pieces

2 teaspoons kosher salt

PAN DE ARROZ

RICE BREAD RINGS

These crunchy, cheesy rice flour rings are originally from a town in the flatlands called Villavicencio, a region with extensive grasslands, cattle ranches, pine-apples, and rice fields. The town is in the heart of the Colombian plains and shares its eastern border with Venezuela, as well as a well-rooted cowboy cul-ture: horses, boots, hats, and rodeo-like festivities that celebrate cattle farming. Colombian cowboys sing about their land, oddly enough, to the tunes of harps and maracas.

Sweet rice flour is made with a sticky rice variety; it doesn't have any added sugar and it is very easy to find in the gluten-free section of any grocery store.

Preheat the oven to 350°F. Line two baking sheets with parchment paper.

Place the cottage cheese in a food processor and mix until smooth.

In a large bowl, combine the rice flour and butter and, working with the tips of your fingers, incorporate the butter into the flour until the texture is sandy and comes together when pressed between your fingers. Add the cottage cheese and salt and stir to combine to form a dough. Add cold water, 1 teaspoon at a time, if the dough appears too dry. (It should have the consistency of Play-Doh.) Cover and allow to rest for 20 minutes.

Turn the rested dough onto a lightly floured surface and divide into four pieces. Take one piece of dough and keep the other three pieces covered with a damp kitchen towel as you work. Cut the first piece into four smaller pieces. Roll each of the smaller pieces out into a ¼-inch-thick rope. You should have 4 ropes in total, each about 18 inches long. Cut each rope into 6-inch strands and then form rings by joining each end together. Repeat this process with the remaining three original pieces of dough.

Place the rings on the prepared baking sheets and bake until golden underneath, 17 to 19 minutes. The rings are ready when they have an amber color on the bottom and a light hue of buttery gold on top. Allow the rings to cool completely before serving. Rice bread rings keep very well stored in an airtight container for up to 2 weeks.

MAKES 16 *PASTELES*

1-pound box frozen puff pastry sheets (my preferred brand is Dufour), thawed

All-purpose flour, for dusting

7 ounces guava or quince paste, cut into 16 squares, ⅛ x 1-inch thick, or 1 cup marmalade of your choice

4 ounces feta cheese, patted dry and cut into 16 squares, ⅛ x 1-inch thick

1 egg, whisked

2 tablespoons Demerara sugar

PASTEL "GLORIA"

GUAVA PASTE & FETA CHEESE PASTRIES

I'm not sure which goddess named Gloria received the honor of this buttery, flaky pastry in her name. Traditionally, a *pastel gloria* is a puff pastry round filled with guava paste, cheese, and, in decadent cases, *arequipe* (dulce de leche). The laminated pastry expands in the oven, creating rippled layers that remind me of the desert mountain stones in Utah. These sweet, crumbly bites go perfectly with a cup of coffee or tea.

Guava and quince paste can be very sticky. For easier cutting, lightly oil or spray your knife with cooking spray.

Preheat the oven to 375°F. Line two baking sheets with parchment paper.

Unfold one of the puff pastry sheets, keeping the second one covered in the refrigerator. (The standard sheet size is an 8 x 8-inch square.) Dust the countertop with flour and roll out the pastry to a 12 x 12-inch square. Cut out 16 discs using a 3-inch round cutter or a drinking glass, and transfer the discs to one of the prepared baking sheets.

Place one piece of guava paste stacked with one piece of cheese in the center of half of the discs. Brush the surrounding outer rim with the egg wash and top with an empty disc. Press the edges with the tips of your fingers, brush with the egg wash, and sprinkle with the Demerara sugar.

Transfer to the oven and bake until puffed up and golden brown, 18 to 20 minutes.

Repeat with the remaining sheet. Serve warm.

FRUITS & JUICES

It took me three years to prepare the first book I authored in Spanish, a full glossary of tropical fruits from A to Z, together with a description of their origin, cultural symbols, use as remedies, songs, and folklore-inspired legends.

Researchers have counted about four hundred different fruit types and local seeds in Colombia.

Since fruit stands populate every part of Colombian life, from countryside kiosks to market stalls, stoplight vendors, hipster bars, and white-cloth restaurants, the country's diverse fruits and their respective salads are also ever present.

Just ask anyone who has visited Colombia: they will speak of the glorious fruits, from *lulo* to *curuba*, from *tamarillo* to *níspero*. They are all vibrant: the reds are exuberant; the yellows, oranges, and greens are so bright, they are almost candescent. *Guanábanas* and *chirimoyas* are fruits with outer layers that resemble alligator skins. The *granadillas* have perfectly contained seeds like pomegranates, except they are yellow on the outside, almost transparent on the inside, and sweet as can be. *Guamas*, in the legume family, have these perfectly pillowy seeds covered with a white floral flesh that seems almost impossible to believe. My friend Debbie—a cheese expert living in Alabama—called it a yogurt fruit. So yeah, picture yogurt pockets in a fruit.

Alas, many of them don't travel well. Think soft shells, small producers, quick ripening, lack of connecting roads. So, some of the most precious fruits have stayed mostly local, with a slowly growing presence in the country's big cities. Because of that, most of their juices are still quite exotic.

The preferred drink for lunch in Colombia is blended fresh fruit with water or milk and sometimes sugar. Actually, the same goes for all other meals of the day in our country. Juice is a must. Always. Never as thick as a smoothie, usually strained through a sieve, frothy fruit juices come in a wide array of colors and flavors, depending on the area. Our coastal cities have juice stands on every other corner, and it is common to replace milk with powdered milk so that vendors don't have to fret with fresh milk going bad.

There is one particular place in Cartagena's old walled city called La Casa del Pandebono, on the corner of the buzzling Calle de la Universidad, where you'll find ten or twelve Oster blenders buzzing, mixing frozen fruit to order. Forget about apple or pomegranate or pineapple juices—brace yourself for *mamey, níspero, lulo, guanábana, curuba, mangostino,* and mango. The orders are called out loud as women speedily and systematically blend, prepare, and pour rivers of fresh velvety fruit juice for awaiting customers.

Thankfully, many of these fruits are frozen by popular Hispanic foods brands and can be found in the freezer section of many Latin and Asian markets around the country.

MARKET FRUIT SALAD

SERVES 8 TO 10

2 small ripe papayas, peeled, seeded, and cut into spears

1 small ripe pineapple, peeled and cut into spears

1 baby seedless watermelon, cut into spears

1 cup *uchuvas* or husk cherries, husks removed

1 small cantaloupe melon, peeled and cut into spears

2 *pitayas* or dragon fruits, peeled and cut into wedges (optional)

Juice of 2 limes

Optional toppings

1 cup shredded *ricotta salata*

2 cups whipped cream

1 cup shredded coconut

A dash of flaky sea salt

To make a proper Colombian fruit salad, you need to forget everything you know about fruit salads: their flavors, composition, and presentation. These salads are mountains of fruit and cream. Remember: more is more.

The fruit salads you can order at stands and in restaurants differ depending on the region of Colombia. Some places will let you make your own fruit selection, while others won't. Some offer sweetened condensed milk or shredded fresh cheese, others will add grated coconut or grounds of Milo (a chocolate and malt powder popular in South America). You may even find them soaked in soda pop, ice cream, or shaved ice. These different mixes and presentations will render different names like the *cholado* in Cali or *salpicón*.

Being the purist that I am when approaching treatment to fruit, I'll go with no toppings for this one. That's not to say you shouldn't indulge in all the toppings you'd like—by all means, please do!

Assemble the papayas, pineapple, watermelon, *uchuvas*, cantaloupe, and *pitayas* on a platter or divide among individual bowls and squeeze the lime juice over the fruit. Add any toppings you fancy. Serve immediately.

SERVES 6 TO 8

24 cups watermelon chunks (1 medium watermelon)

1 cup freshly squeezed lime juice

6 cups ice

8 cups ice-cold club soda

PATILLAZO

WATERMELON & LIME PUNCH

Barranquilla is a modern sprawling city that sits at the mouth of the Magdalena River, overlooking the Caribbean Sea. Referred to as La Arenosa (the Sandy One), Barranquilla hosts the country's largest yearly carnival, mixing African, Indigenous, and many other traditions. It's actually one of the world's largest carnivals, although it remains lesser known to international tourists. People take over the streets, dress up in costumes, and dance, drink, and eat the night away, carrying on all the next day and into the night and day again.

The *patillazo* came to me on a steamy Barranquilla afternoon. I was in meetings during a quick visit to the city and lunch was distant. Dehydration, an understatement. I pulled over onto the sidewalk underneath a tin roof where I found a crowd of schoolchildren, chatting and joking away as they dipped their spoons into tall cups of crushed watermelon with tons of lime and ice. The watermelon pieces had been steeping in the lime juice long enough for its flavor to become more intense, the chunks of watermelon extra supple. It was the perfect antidote to my exhaustion and hunger.

In this sense, there is nothing extraordinary about this recipe except the way the flavors come together so seamlessly, making for a delightful midsummer drink.

Place the watermelon, lime juice, and ice in a large pitcher. Using a wooden spoon, stir and partially muddle the watermelon. Refrigerate for at least 30 minutes. Right before serving, top with the club soda and serve in ball glasses with a spoon.

SERVES 8 TO 10

1 (14-ounce) can hominy corn, drained and rinsed

1 very ripe pineapple, peeled and cut into ¼-inch cubes

2 pounds thawed frozen *lulo* pulp, or 6 green apples, cut into ¼-inch cubes

½ teaspoon ground cloves

1 teaspoon ground cinnamon

¼ cup ground panela or brown sugar

1 teaspoon Angostura or orange bitters

CHAMPÚS

PINEAPPLE, LULO & SWEET CORN SLUSHY

This popular drink was born in the city of Cali, birthplace of professional salsa dancing. It is served out of pushcarts topped with large glass fish-tank-style vessels filled with chunks of pineapple, *lulo* (see page 17), corn, and bitter orange tree leaves, and spiced with cinnamon and cloves. Floating icebergs chill the whole mix, before it is ladled into tall cups and served with a spoon and a straw; the former is used to catch the pieces of fruit and the latter to suck the rest up.

The traditional drink is sweetened with panela, but I've lowered the amount of added sugar significantly. Also, since most of us (sadly) don't have a bitter orange tree in the backyard, orange bitters or Angostura bitters are a good substitute.

Spread the hominy on a cutting board and roughly chop it. Transfer to a pitcher with the pineapple, *lulo*, cloves, and cinnamon, and refrigerate. Meanwhile, dissolve the *panela* in a few tablespoons of boiling water. Allow to cool and add to the pitcher. Cover with ice-cold water and add the bitters. Adjust the sweetness to taste and serve chilled in tall glasses with a spoon.

SERVES 4

4 tablespoons ground panela

1-inch piece ginger root, peeled and thinly sliced

¼ cup fresh lemon verbena or mint leaves, torn

1 cup cubed part-skim mozzarella cheese

AGUA DE PANELA CON CIDRÓN, JENGIBRE Y QUESO

PANELA, LEMON VERBENA & GINGER INFUSION

The main road that connects one of the major ports of entry on the Pacific coast to the rest of the country has a famous stretch called La Linea. It's a winding mountain pass in the central branch of the Andes, with a drop so narrow and intense, it's hard not to get weak in the knees when looking off to the side. Also, keep in mind that the road is usually shared with eighteen-wheelers that have to take tight turns, often making more than one attempt to make the curve, pulling back and forth, and narrowly making it through these narrow bends.

Hanging off the cliff, before the steepest section of the pass, there is a famous roadside restaurant called La Paloma. This precarious cement house with concrete walls, coral red metal doors, and rustic furniture serves all kinds of heartwarming foods. My favorite is breakfast: *Caldo de Costilla* (page 36), beans with rice and plantains (page 142), and, among many other options, the *agua de panela con queso*.

The infusion is made with unrefined sugar and is spruced up with a mozzarella-like local cheese. Yes, you read correctly: the cheese goes inside and becomes chewy and melty. In between sips of the hot sweet liquid, you fish the cheese out with a spoon. This may be an acquired taste, I know, but I have added ginger and lemon verbena to my version in an attempt to elevate the flavors a bit. The cheese is optional, but I do dare you to try it. It gives a new meaning to the word "heartwarming."

Place the *panela*, ginger, and lemon verbena leaves in a medium saucepan. Cover with water and bring to a boil over high heat. Stir until the *panela* dissolves. Cover, turn off the heat, and allow the flavors to steep for 5 to 10 minutes. Strain into cups and serve the cheese on the side or in the cups.

CHICHA DE ARROZ, ALMENDRA & PIMIENTA DULCE

RICE, ALMOND & ALLSPICE CHICHA

SERVES 6

½ cup long-grain
white rice

6 cups unsweetened
almond milk

1 teaspoon whole allspice

2 cinnamon sticks

Coconut sugar

Ice

Decades ago, I was the field producer for celebrity chef Leonor Espinosa's documentary on Colombian foods. We went along the Caribbean coast in search of heirloom techniques and fading cooking methods with a camera crew and ended up at a *ranchería*: a reservation-type camp in the Guajira peninsula, mostly inhabited by indigenous tribes called the Guayús. Women wearing long colorful cotton kaftans, wool pom-pom sandals, and stern looks invited us for a meal of goat braised in blood and rice called *friche*.

After twenty-one days on the road in hellishly hot weather, and little access to clean water—and having tasted all sorts of foraged ingredients like iguana eggs, fish cooked on an open fire in Palenque, and hand-pulled cheese from Mompox—I had what one could call a queasy stomach. As much as I wanted to be open and adventurous, the goat dish gracefully served to us by the Guayús wasn't going down well. One of the women must have seen my pale face and sweaty brow, so she brought over a white drink, saying: "Here, to settle you." I took a tiny sip while politely giving her a tight smile. Then, the taste hit me. It was sublime. Creamy rice milk, very lightly spiced. It comforted both my belly and my soul.

This recipe is a reconstruction of that moment I'll never forget: a memory from my early days of culinary research has brought me here.

Place the rice and almond milk in a medium saucepan. Wrap the allspice and cinnamon sticks in a piece of cheesecloth or a tea filter and add to the pot. Bring to a boil over high heat, lower the heat, and continue cooking, stirring now and then, until the rice softens, about 25 minutes.

Remove the pot from the heat and allow to cool. Remove the cheesecloth packet, and then transfer the rice and liquid to the blender. Process until smooth. Add coconut sugar to taste and ice. I personally like leaving a bit of a chunky texture, but it is up to you. Serve very cold.

STREET FOOD

It is 9 a.m. and a light drizzle covers the streets of Bogotá. I walk past boutiques of local designers, world-renowned labels, and art galleries, and right there I stumble into a Renault 4 parked on the street. It's mint green and has its trunk wide open, displaying a setup with coffee thermoses, cut mangoes, cups filled with papayas and watermelon slices, one large fresh OJ press, crackers, candy, snacks, and, yes, cigarettes. Its owner, Mr. Juan Lozano, wears a robe to match his makeshift mobile "shop" and offers me coffee, sweetened with panela and flavored with cinnamon and cloves.

Mr. Lozano is doing what we call *el rebusque*, the colloquial way of referring to the act of making a living however possible, scrambling and doing what it takes. Hustling. It often results in creative food endeavors: making empanadas for sale; setting up a dessert stand on the weekends (see *Merengón de Fresa*, page 128); bike front racks hacked into moving griddles for eggs, arepas, and sausages; milk crates with wheels attached and pulled by a rope to deliver perfectly packaged homemade lunches at offices around entire neighborhoods.

There isn't an attraction in our country that will not include a food hustler, *ahem,* vendor. For example, one can always trust that a warm basket of tamales will come to the car window in a country road traffic jam or that you'll find blackberry preserves slathered over fresh cheese as you hike up the Monserrate mountain path, used by pilgrims and penitents. Most corners of this steep trail feature a person grilling arepas on an open fire or preparing wafer discs filled with *arequipe* and cream. We call these *obleas*.

I celebrate street vendors who, day in and day out, walk thousands of steps no matter the weather, tending to their stands and selling their handmade foods. All over the world it is a form of life, a way to survive, and a cultural treasure that gives the streets texture and soul.

COCKTAIL DE CAMARÓN "PLAYERO"

BEACHY SHRIMP COCKTAIL

SERVES 6 TO 8

1 lemon, cut in half

1 bay leaf

2 teaspoons kosher salt, plus more for cooking the shrimp

1½ pounds small shrimp, peeled and deveined

½ cup nice-quality mayonnaise

3 tablespoons Dijon mustard

½ cup ketchup

2 shallots, minced

Juice of 2 limes

Freshly ground black pepper

Hot sauce of your choice

Saltine crackers

Beach food is a bit questionable to me. There are so many elements at stake. Sandy hands, salty lips, sea breeze, hats to hold up, and bellies to suck in. But those white coolers strapped over a vendor's shoulder can be promising.

Creamy, savory, and meaty shrimp cocktail as simple and delicious as it can be. Nothing fussy or complex. A street food that can be found in old zinc *caseta* stands where your cocktail (small, medium, or large) is prepared by squirting mayo, ketchup, hot sauce, and onions right into a plastic cup. A vigorous stir performed by the vendor who glances at you in search of a nod of approval on more spice or less lemon juice.

If possible, ask your local seafood market for fresh, never frozen shrimp, which are sweet and wonderfully firm in texture.

Fill a medium pot with water, squeeze the cut lemon into it, and add the lemon halves along with the bay leaf. Season liberally with salt and bring to a boil over high heat. Meanwhile, set a bowl of ice water near the stove.

Add the shrimp to the boiling water and cook until they begin to turn pink, 3 to 4 minutes. Remove the cooked shrimp with a spider or slotted spoon, and place in the ice water to stop them from cooking.

In a medium bowl, combine the mayonnaise, mustard, ketchup, shallots, lime juice, salt, pepper to taste, and hot sauce of your choice. Stir to combine to form a homogenous sauce. Add the cold cooked shrimp and stir to coat completely. Taste and adjust the seasoning if needed. Serve in small cups or bowls topped with saltine crackers.

MAKES 6 HOT DOGS

½ cup ketchup

½ cup mayonnaise

6 beef hot dogs

Spicy mustard

½ cup sliced cornichons
(cut into rounds)

½ cup minced pineapple

½ cup minced white onion

One 5-ounce bag potato
chips, crushed in the bag

6 hot dog top-split buns,
preferably from a local
bakery

PERRO CALIENTE CON TODO

THE EVERYTHING HOT DOG

More is more. Maximalists know it. Colombian hot dog aficionados know it, too.

On late nights after drinks, partying, concerts, and sport events, the place to go is either the hotdog stands outside whatever venue you danced the night away or the nearest gas station that has a hotd og stand in it.

Unlike their American counterparts, Colombian hot dog vendors have maximized their product by adding as many toppings as the bun and wiener can possibly take. The list starts conservatively: ketchup, mustard, radishes, pickles, and melted cheese. Then it spirals out of control: Russian dressing, bacon, lettuce, pineapple preserves, coleslaw, potato chips, hard-boiled eggs—even quail eggs make it into the mix.

My favorite topping is by far crushed potato chips. My mouth waters a bit as I type. The texture is a superb contrast to the soft sweet bun, the charred sausage, and the heavy sauces. The cornichons in this recipe are my own addition. I prefer the tiny flavorful pieces to the sweetened relish. It is all about how you set it up. A fun topping bar with many options and good-quality buns really upgrades the spread.

Preheat the grill to medium-high heat. Oil the grate lightly, and grill the hot dogs, turning now and then, until they have grill marks all over, 8 to 10 minutes. Meanwhile, set up the toppings. Place the ketchup and mayonnaise in a medium bowl and mix to combine. Place the remaining toppings into bowls.

Warm up the buns on the grill if you like. Assemble the hot dogs as usual, and top with the ketchup-mayonnaise sauce, mustard, cornichons, pineapple, onion, and crushed chips, to your liking.

Gaeleen Quinn

Gaeleen is smart, direct, sweet, and a loyal friend. She has passionately worked in the food industry for more than twenty years in different capacities, always focused on one goal: food as a means to promote positive change. An industrial engineer with an MBA from SDA Bocconi in Milan, her love for food has taken her around the world, working for high-end restaurants and top food producers in a diverse range of strategic and operational duties.

Her multiple endeavors include the Bogotá Wine and Food Festival (a yearly gathering of the world's best chefs in Colombia to raise funds for local youth) and a hospitality business consulting agency called Q&A that, for the last decade, has helped chefs, restaurateurs, and companies create socially conscious, profitable concepts.

In March 2020, amid a global pandemic, Gaeleen created Ask Chefs Anything, a campaign whose aim was to raise awareness and funds for immigrant workers most impacted by the COVID crisis within the US restaurant world. This effort started in New York City and has been replicated in Los Angeles, Philadelphia, Miami, St. Louis, Chicago, Dallas, San Francisco, Nashville, and Houston. It cumulatively raised over $220,000.

Today, Gaeleen is the East Coast director of Too Good To Go, the world's number one app for fighting food waste.

We Colombianas are proud to call her one of our own.

In this chapter, I wanted to share some simpler, everyday recipes inspired by the places, stories, and flavors deeply ingrained in my food philosophy. It's mostly the seasons that dictate what I prepare, though the actual process is always engraved with the *sazón* of my heritage.

The recipes that follow aren't quintessentially Colombian plates—they are my adaptation of influences borne out of years of work in the food world, the way I eat, and what inspires me. The Soupy Pearl Barley with Mushrooms & Chorizo (page 250) warms any winter with the memory of Villa de Leiva's balmy December winds. Rice & Toasted Angel Hair Pilaf with Ground Beef, Capers & Raisins (page 253) is a journey in time straight to my Lebanese grandmother's patio, under the shade of a mango tree. The scallop and ripe tomato salad (page 241) gets richer with the addition of *chicharrón* and it is one I think about when it is not around.

I hope these recipes can become part of your repertoire, just as they are a part of mine.

SERVES 4 TO 6

4 pomelos or pink grapefruits, peeled and cut into segments (use your hands to separate the meat from the white membrane)

1 (14-ounce) jar hearts of palm, cut into spears

2 medium watermelon radishes, peeled and thinly sliced

Juice of 2 limes

1 jalapeño, seeded, deveined, and thinly sliced

3 tablespoons fruity extra-virgin olive oil

Flaky sea salt and freshly ground black pepper

½ cup chopped cilantro, for garnish

CEVICHE DE PALMITO & POMELO

TANGY HEART OF PALM & CITRUS CEVICHE

This is a refreshing and delicate salad that I relish serving as a sophisticated appetizer. It's just so easy. The soft and hot pinks alongside the whites and gentle greens make the salad very chic. If pomelos aren't in season, replace them with pink grapefruit. The hearts of palm play up a meaty texture that is both satisfying and clean. I prefer jarred to canned hearts of palm; the texture tends to be firmer and the brine less salty.

Although grown all along the Equator (mainly in Brazil), hearts of palm have a strong meaning for Colombians. These stocky, short palms have become one of the chosen replacements for illegal crops, part of the government's strategy to give communities a safer way of life.

In a large bowl, gently toss together the pomelos, hearts of palm, radishes, lime juice, jalapeño, and oil, and season with salt and pepper. Allow the ceviche to marinate for 10 to 20 minutes. This allows for the citrus and hearts of palm to absorb the flavors. When ready to serve, transfer to a platter along with the juices and garnish with the cilantro.

SERVES 4 TO 6

1½ pounds large sea scallops, sliced into ⅛- to ¼-inch rounds

2 medium garlic cloves, grated or finely chopped

4 teaspoons kosher salt, divided

Juice of 2 limes

12 small ripe tomatoes, halved

1 small red onion, thinly sliced

2 teaspoons sumac

Freshly ground black pepper

4 large ears corn, husked

1 tablespoon extra-virgin olive oil

1 cup small basil leaves

½ cup chopped chives

2 cups meaty baked pork rinds (*chicharrónes*)

ENSALADA DE VIEIRAS & MAZORCA ASADA

GRILLED CORN SALAD WITH SCALLOPS & JUICY TOMATOES

The smoky scent of roasting corn on the cob from a cart, slathered with margarine and sprinkled with salt by the vendor, usually envelops the winding mountain-side roads all over Colombia. Points of pilgrimage are hubs for these charred golden cobs.

The local variety of corn typically used has large, sturdy kernels that swell up and caramelize when cooked over the rumbling coals of an open fire. I used to crave them. I still do.

This salad is summer in a bowl, with tomatoes and herbs at their peak. An optional addition is a touch of salty, crispy *chicharrón* (pork rinds). My favorite brand is called Epic and they are baked, as opposed to fried, which makes them a lot less greasy.

Add the scallops to a non-reactive bowl. Place the garlic and 2 teaspoons of the salt on a cutting board, and with the blade of your knife at a 45-degree angle, crush the garlic and salt together to make a paste. Add to the scallops and pour in the lime juice. Stir so that the garlic and salt paste coat the scallops well. Marinate in the refrigerator for at least 20 minutes.

Meanwhile, preheat a grill or cast-iron grill pan over medium-high heat.

In a separate bowl, toss the tomatoes, onion, sumac, the remaining 2 teaspoons salt, and black pepper to taste. Allow for the flavors to develop at room temperature while you grill the corn.

Brush the corn with the olive oil. Grill, turning often, until charred and softened, 6 to 8 minutes. Remove from the grill and set aside to cool slightly. Slice off the kernels with a serrated knife, add to the tomatoes, and stir in the marinated scallops. Finish by sprinkling with the basil and chives, and top with the *chicharrón* pieces. Serve right away.

**SERVES 4 AS A MAIN COURSE,
6 AS AN APPETIZER**

½ cup white wine vinegar

2 garlic cloves, grated

¾ cup plus 1 tablespoon olive oil, divided

2 teaspoons flaky sea salt, plus more as needed

Freshly ground black pepper

2 pounds calamari tails and tentacles, cleaned

1 pound frozen yuca, thawed, vein removed, cut into 2-inch-long sticks

½ cup cilantro leaves, roughly chopped

2 tablespoons chopped chives

Lemon wedges, to serve

ENSALADA DE CALAMAR

GRILLED CALAMARI SALAD WITH CRISPY YUCA & LEMONY DRESSING

This salad can be served as a full meal in warmer months. Prepping the components in advance makes it effortless to toss together, and the dressing tastes even better after it sits for a bit. The key to having the right texture when preparing calamari is to cook them quickly over high heat, which results in a meaty, tender bite with a lovely briny taste.

Yuca is one of those starches that has always had my heart. It's multifaceted and can be prepared in so many ways: boiled and served with a spoonful of *suero* (crème fraîche); deep-fried in French-fry fashion with a squeeze of lime; grated into *Enyucado* (page 272); or wrapped in a corn husk, served with a slab of *costeño* cheese—salty farmer cheese—as a *bollo* (bun).

Preheat the oven to 375°F.

Place the vinegar and garlic in a bowl large enough to hold the calamari, and whisk as you slowly pour in the ¾ cup oil to emulsify. Season with the salt and pepper to taste. Pour 1 cup of the marinade into a separate large bowl and set aside. Add the calamari to the bowl with the remaining marinade and toss to coat in the emulsion. Let marinate for 25 to 30 minutes in the refrigerator.

Prepare the grill for high heat or preheat a cast-iron grill pan over high heat.

Meanwhile, place the yuca sticks on a baking sheet, drizzle with the remaining 1 tablespoon oil, toss to coat, and season thoroughly with salt. Bake in the oven until golden brown, 30 to 35 minutes. Remove from the oven and set aside.

Remove the calamari from the marinade and discard the liquid. Place the calamari on the preheated grill and cook quickly in a single layer, turning once, about 2 minutes per side. Transfer to the reserved marinade, add the yuca sticks, and stir to combine. To serve, transfer to a platter and garnish with the cilantro, chives, a generous grind of black pepper, and the lemon wedges.

SERVES 4 TO 6

12 small, organic air-chilled chicken thighs, bone in, skin removed (about 3 pounds)

4 teaspoons kosher salt, divided

Freshly ground black pepper

1 (14.5-ounce) can full-fat coconut milk, chilled (you'll use the liquid fat layer as your starting oil) See page 11

3 sweet chilies, such as Cubanelle or sweet Italian

1 large shallot, cut in half lengthwise

4 garlic cloves, grated

1 jalapeño, seeded, deveined, and finely chopped

2 cups chicken broth

1 plantain, very ripe, peeled and cut into ½-inch cubes

Juice of 1 large lime

1 cup roughly chopped cilantro leaves

White Rice (page 113) (optional)

POLLO GUISADO EN COCO Y AJÍ CRIOLLO

CHICKEN BRAISED IN COCONUT & SWEET CHILIES

On cold, wintry nights this is a go-to recipe that is both comforting and delicious. I adore when the toasty scent of coconut permeates the kitchen.

When buying chicken, look for the words "organic air-chilled" on the label. Simply put, air-chilled is a process in which chicken is cooled with blasts of cold air, and since there is no added moisture it retains all of its flavor and juiciness, leaving less room for contamination, and the chicken doesn't need to be washed—you don't want to add extra flavorless liquid.

This recipe provides plenty of leftovers and the chicken is even better the next day.

Remove the chicken thighs from their packaging, pat dry, and place on a tray. Season with 2 teaspoons of the salt and with the pepper to taste and set aside. Heat a large cast-iron skillet—if you don't have one, a 12-inch stainless steel skillet with a lid works well—until it is piping hot. Add 1 tablespoon coconut fat from the top layer of the can and half of the chicken thighs. Sear the thighs without touching them (you will be tempted to check if they are browning—don't!) until golden brown, about 6 minutes per side. Add another 1 tablespoon of coconut fat and finish searing the remaining thighs.

Meanwhile, put the sweet chilies and the halved shallot on a grill pan over high heat or directly over the flame on an arepa griddle or comal. Turn as they blacken so all areas of the chilies and shallot are charred. Transfer to a cutting board and allow to cool. There is no need to peel the chilies. Simply remove the seeds and finely chop.

Discard all but 1 tablespoon of the fat from the skillet used to brown the chicken. Turn the heat to high and add the chopped chilies, shallot, garlic, and jalapeño. Cook, stirring with a wooden spoon and scraping all the flavored golden bits remaining from the chicken, until fragrant, about 1 minute. Deglaze the pan with the chicken broth, season with the remaining 2 teaspoons salt, and bring to a boil. Return the seared chicken to the skillet and snuggle the pieces into a single layer. Bring to a boil, cover, turn the heat down to a gentle but constant simmer, and cook for 35 minutes.

Uncover, drizzle in the coconut milk, and add the plantain cubes. The chicken pieces will still be very snug but should have shrunk a little so you will be able to incorporate the coconut milk and submerge the plantain pieces. Cover and continue to simmer until the sauce appears slightly thicker and the plantains are fully cooked but still hold their shape, about 10 minutes. Before serving, add the lime juice. Taste and adjust the seasoning if needed.

Divide the rice, if using, among serving plates and top with one or two chicken pieces. Ladle the sauce over each plate and garnish with the cilantro.

SERVES 6

1 (2½-pound) center-cut pork loin

2 teaspoons kosher salt

Freshly ground black pepper

2 tablespoons canola oil

¼ cup dark rum

⅓ cup tamarind paste, seeds removed

2 small red onions, quartered through the root end

2 cups chicken broth

3 tablespoon grated panela or dark brown sugar

1 tablespoon grated fresh horseradish, or 1 tablespoon prepared horseradish

½ cup mint leaves, chopped

LOMITO DE CERDO AL TAMARINDO Y MENTA

TAMARIND-BRAISED PORK LOIN WITH MINT

This is the juiciest pork loin ever. The secret lies in the acid from the tamarind and the slow braise—paired together, the meat becomes unbelievably tender. I learned this method from author Caroline Chambers while styling her book *Just Married*, and I adapted it to feature flavors from my home. Tamarind paste can be purchased in the Asian condiment section of the supermarket as a block or in a jar. I couldn't help but think about the scene in *The Autumn of the Patriarch* where the main character "lived and slept his siesta under the shade of a tamarind tree."

Preheat the oven to 325°F.

Season the pork with the salt and pepper to taste. Let stand at room temperature for 15 to 30 minutes, to lose the cold from the refrigerator and for the salt to do its magic.

Heat the oil in a 10-inch cast-iron skillet or a heavy-bottom sauté pan. Add the roast and sear on all sides, 15 to 20 minutes, until a dark golden crust forms.

Remove the roast using tongs and transfer to a rimmed platter. Turn the heat to medium, deglaze the pan with the rum, and bring to a simmer, scraping up the brown crusty bits with the back of a wooden spoon. Cook until the alcohol evaporates, about 45 seconds. Add the tamarind paste, onions, chicken broth, and *panela*, and bring to a simmer. Return the pork to the pan. Carefully transfer the skillet to the preheated oven and roast for 40 to 50 minutes, until the internal temperature on a meat thermometer reaches 145°F.

Remove the pork loin from the sauce and transfer to a rimmed serving platter. Tent with foil and allow to rest for 10 to 15 minutes. Meanwhile, finish the sauce: stir the horseradish and mint leaves into the sauce. Taste for seasoning and add a bit more salt if needed. To serve, cut the pork into medallions and spoon the sauce and onions over the loin.

SERVES 4 TO 6

2 whole scallions,
thinly sliced on the bias

1 small jalapeño, seeded,
deveined, and finely chopped
(1 tablespoon)

Juice of 2 limes

2 teaspoons flaky sea salt

1 teaspoon ground coriander

Freshly ground black pepper

2 tablespoons extra-virgin
olive oil

2 cara cara oranges, peeled,
cut into ¼-inch rounds

2 blood oranges, peeled,
cut into ¼-inch rounds

2 tablespoons cilantro leaves

2 tablespoons mint leaves

2 tablespoons chopped chives

CUYACO

ORANGE & SCALLION SALAD

The upside of January is citrus. During my college years, I remember a particularly cold -30°F winter day in Vermont, when I spotted the headline of the local paper, which read: "Orange You Glad It's January?" At that temperature, I was not happy, but I was certainly glad I had *cuyaco*: a savory orange salad from the Cauca Valley region that always brightens my day. The addition of blood oranges—which were a novelty to me—made it even better. This is a lovely side served with grilled chicken or seafood.

In a bowl, whisk together the scallions, jalapeño, lime juice, salt, coriander, and black pepper to taste. Slowly pour in the oil in a steady stream to emulsify.

Arrange the cara cara and blood oranges on a rimmed serving platter, drizzle with the dressing, and allow to marinate for at least 10 minutes before serving.

Sprinkle with the cilantro, mint, and chives and serve.

SERVES 4

For the mushroom broth

1 tablespoon extra-virgin olive oil

2 shallots, sliced

1 pound cremini mushrooms, quartered

3 stems fresh thyme

2 teaspoons cumin seeds

1 tablespoon tomato paste

1 cup sherry or red wine

8 cups beef broth

4 cups water

Kosher salt and freshly ground black pepper

For the barley

1 tablespoon olive oil

1 large yellow onion, chopped

1 leek, white and light green parts only, washed and sliced into ¼-inch-thick rounds

1 cup pearl barley, rinsed

6 ounces dried spicy (or mild) Spanish chorizo, cut into ¼-inch rounds

2 teaspoons lemon zest

1 tablespoon lemon juice

CEBADA PERLADA CALDOSA CON CHAMPIÑONES Y CHORIZO

SOUPY PEARL BARLEY WITH MUSHROOMS & CHORIZO

Pearl barley soup is often made in the cold-weather farmland region of Boyacá, well above sea level, where the dense green rolling hills are covered with lilac and white flowers, with the capacity to grow potatoes, beans, and grains. This traditional soup has a minestrone-like preparation. It's a concoction with everything on hand: grains, vegetables, herbs, chorizo, and whatever you can find in your crisper. My adaptation uses spicy Spanish chorizo for a kick. This makes for a well-rounded, comforting meal.

Make the mushroom broth: Heat the oil in a large pot over medium-high heat, add the shallots, and sauté until the shallots become fragrant and begin to soften without getting any color, 5 to 6 minutes. Add the mushrooms and stir to coat with the oil. Cook about 5 minutes, stirring as the mushrooms sweat and soften, about 4 minutes. Add the thyme, cumin seeds, and tomato paste and stir to combine. Cook, stirring with a wooden spoon, until fragrant, about 1 minute.

Deglaze the pot with the sherry and bring to a boil; cook until the alcohol evaporates, 1 to 2 minutes. Pour in the broth and water, season with salt and pepper to taste, and bring to a boil. Lower the heat to medium and simmer for 25 minutes. Remove from the heat and strain through a fine-mesh sieve. Discard the vegetables and pour the broth back into the pot over low heat.

Make the barley: While the broth simmers, heat the oil in a medium Dutch oven or other heavy-bottom saucepan over medium-high heat. Add the onion and leek and cook, stirring, until softened, 6 to 8 minutes. Add the barley and stir to incorporate, making sure that all the barley grains are coated with the oil. Add 3 cups of the mushroom broth and bring to a boil, stirring now and then with a wooden spoon; cook until the liquid is almost all absorbed, about 15 minutes. Add 2 more cups broth and stir. Continue adding broth and stirring until you have no more broth left and the barley is al dente, 35 to 40 minutes.

Finally, stir in the chorizo, lemon zest, and lemon juice. Carefully taste and season with salt and pepper. Serve right away.

SERVES 4 TO 6

For the rice

2 tablespoons olive oil

2 ounces angel hair pasta, broken into 1-inch pieces

1 cup long-grain white rice, washed until the water runs clear

2 teaspoons kosher salt, plus more as needed

For the *picadillo*

1 tablespoon olive oil

4 garlic cloves, grated

1 small yellow onion, finely diced (about 1 cup)

1 pound 90% lean ground beef

1 teaspoon ground cinnamon

½ teaspoon ground allspice

Kosher salt

½ pound Swiss chard, stems cut into ¼-inch slices and leaves chopped

3 tablespoons capers

⅓ cup green pimento olives, sliced crosswise into rounds

½ cup black raisins

2 cups small cherry tomatoes, halved

1 cup chicken broth or water

½ cup fresh lime juice

½ cup plain Greek yogurt

4 cups small mint leaves

Freshly ground black pepper

ARROZ CON FIDEOS Y CARNE MOLIDA

RICE AND TOASTED ANGEL HAIR PILAF WITH GROUND BEEF, CAPERS & RAISINS

Rice pilaf, which is a staple in many nations in the Middle East, West Indies, and Africa (each with its own distinct version), appears again and again in my country's day-to-day cuisine—from cheap lunch specials in the middle of a busy weekday to the backs of the stoves at grand estates in the Sopó Valley. I'm a tad uncertain of the exact genesis, but this fluffy rice with brown noodles is a common lunch in Colombian homes.

To make it a full meal, I propose a savory, salty, and sweet beef picadillo with capers, raisins, cinnamon, and Swiss chard. The tomatoes burst, juicing up the sauce, and the combination is homey and comforting.

Make the rice: Heat the oil in a medium *caldero* or heavy-bottom pot. Add the pasta pieces and toast, stirring constantly so that the pieces brown evenly to an amber color, 3 to 4 minutes. Stir in the rice, combining it with the toasted pasta. Quickly cover with 2¼ cups water and add the salt. Bring to a boil over high heat and, once the water is almost completely evaporated, lower the heat and cover. Cook until the water has evaporated and the rice is fluffy, 14 to 16 minutes. Hold the temptation to stir the rice as it is cooking, as this will make it sticky—not in a good way.

While the rice is cooking, fire up the meat!

Make the *picadillo*: Add the oil to a large skillet along with the garlic and onion—I prefer starting the cooking in a cold pan so the garlic and onion don't burn upon hitting the hot oil. Turn the heat to medium-high and cook, stirring with a wooden spoon, until the garlic and onion begin to soften and become sweetly fragrant, 3 to 4 minutes. Add the beef, cinnamon, allspice, and a good pinch of salt and stir, breaking up the ground beef pieces and incorporating the spices into the onion mixture. Cook, stirring now and then, until the beef is no longer red and some pieces take on a caramelized color, 2 to 3 minutes. Fold in the Swiss chard stems, capers, olives, raisins, and tomatoes. Continue cooking over medium-low heat until the tomatoes begin to blister and the Swiss chard stems are tender, 4 to 5 minutes. Pour in the broth and add the Swiss chard leaves and lime juice. Cover and cook until the leaves wilt and the mixture is bubbly, about 5 minutes.

To serve, scoop the rice into individual bowls, and top each one with the beef and 1 tablespoon yogurt. Garnish with the mint leaves and a couple grinds of black pepper and enjoy.

SERVES 6 TO 8

1½ pounds very ripe papaya, peeled, seeded, and cubed (about 4 cups)

1 pound ripe red heirloom tomatoes, cored and cubed

1 small red onion, chopped

2 teaspoons ground achiote or sweet paprika

Juice of 3 limes (⅓ cup)

4 garlic cloves, smashed

1½ cups cubed day-old baguette (crust removed)

1 teaspoon sea salt, plus more to taste

½ cup fruity olive oil

1½ cups ice water, plus more as needed

1 medium leek (white and light green parts only), sliced into ¼-inch rounds

4 tablespoons extra-virgin olive oil, divided

Freshly ground black pepper

½ cup small Thai basil leaves or regular basil

Basil blossoms (optional, but very pretty)

GAZPACHO PICANTE DE PAPAYA & PUERROS

SPICY PAPAYA & CHARRED LEEK GAZPACHO

I cannot wait for the weather to be warm enough to have an excuse to make chilled soup. Not only is it a delicious way to cool down, but it also makes for a light meal or a fabulous appetizer. The many ways to serve gazpacho make it a pure joy to prepare: pour into small vintage juice glasses, espresso cups, or teacups to sip.

The success of this recipe is built on the ripeness of the papaya and tomatoes. These flavors make the soup!

Place the papaya, tomatoes, onion, achiote, lime juice, garlic, bread, salt, and fruity olive oil in a large nonreactive bowl (stainless steel or ceramic-lined; not copper, cast iron, or aluminum). Stir to combine and marinate for 30 minutes to 1 hour— the flavors will develop wonderfully.

In the meantime, make the leek garnish. Pat the leek dry and place in a small bowl. Add 2 tablespoons of the extra-virgin olive oil, and sprinkle with salt and pepper to taste. Mix well. Heat a large cast-iron skillet or grill pan over high heat until it is very hot. Place the leek in the skillet and cook for 20 to 30 seconds, until nicely browned and crisp on the bottom. Turn the leek over using kitchen tongs and cook for 30 seconds more. Set aside.

To finish the soup, place the marinated ingredients in a Vitamix or NutriBullet and blend for 1 minute, or until the soup is silky. Add the 1½ cups ice water and blend. Add more ice water as needed until the soup reaches a silky-smooth consistency.

Serve in small soup bowls or small glasses. Garnish with the leek, Thai basil leaves, the remaining 2 tablespoons extra-virgin olive oil, and basil blossoms, if using.

YUCCA PEPPERED CRACKERS

MAKES ABOUT 40 CRACKERS

1½ cups cassava or yucca flour, plus a bit more for dusting

¼ cup cubed unsalted butter, room temperature

1 teaspoon kosher salt, divided

¾ cup plain 2% Greek yogurt

2 teaspoons freshly ground coarse black pepper

¼ cup lukewarm water

2 teaspoons ground turmeric, divided

2 tablespoons olive oil, for brushing

½ cup leaves of fresh herbs: parsley, tarragon, or thyme

Marbled with yellow turmeric and flecked with black pepper, these crackers are addictive and super-easy to make. I like to serve them as an accompaniment for hummus, gazpacho, or a fresh salad, or paired with cheese and charcuterie for an afternoon snack.

Preheat the oven to 400°F.

Line two baking sheets with parchment paper.

Place the flour, butter, salt, yogurt, pepper, and water in the bowl of a food processor. Pulse several times until a smooth dough forms. Add a bit more water, 1 tablespoon at a time, if the dough appears dry. This dough cannot be overworked, so there is no need to worry.

Transfer the dough onto a clean surface dusted with a dash of cassava flour, and divide it into 4 pieces. Flatten each piece of dough into a disc and add a sprinkle ½ teaspoon turmeric on the surface, then sprinkle with the herbs. Knead the dough to incorporate the powder with a marbling effect. Using a rolling pin, roll out each piece of dough into ⅛-inch-thick oval pieces and cut into whatever shape you desire—rounds, squares, or triangles. Arrange the crackers on the prepared baking sheets, about ½ inch apart. Pierce each cracker with a fork so it doesn't inflate, and bake for 3 to 4 minutes, until slightly golden and crisp. Flip over with metal tongs and bake for another 2 to 3 minutes, until crisp on the other side.

Transfer the crackers to a rack to cool completely. Serve immediately or store for up to a week in a tightly sealed container.

SERVES 4 TO 6

1 whole bone-in chicken breast (both halves), skin removed

8 cups water

2 teaspoons kosher salt

1 bay leaf

2 medium carrots, cut into ½-inch rounds

2 cups cubed butternut squash (½-inch cubes)

1 cup fava beans, shelled, thawed if frozen

1 small leek (white and light green parts), washed and cut into ¼-inch rounds

½ cup fine bulgur

Freshly ground black pepper

Zest and juice of 1 lemon

Fresh cilantro, for garnish

CUCHUCO DE TRIGO CON POLLITO Y LIMÓN

LEMONY BULGUR FARMER'S CHICKEN SOUP

When I think of Boyacá, I think virgin wool sweaters; flowing black braids; tubers, roots, and grains; and steep mountains with vast potato fields below them, bathing in the morning fog and dew. This geography demands so much leg strength that some of the best cyclists in the world have been born and raised right there. Think Lucho, Nairo, and Egan. Google them.

Cuchuco de trigo is a hearty soup usually made with pork spine, bulgur, and whatever vegetables are available: carrots, potatoes, cabbage, onions, fava beans, and peas. Since pork spine can feel like a commitment on any given Tuesday evening, I replaced it with chicken. Some will definitely frown upon this exchange, but it is just as delicious, and the bones from the chicken breast flavor the broth. The lemon zest and juice enliven the flavors in the way only acid can, making this a satisfying meal.

Place the chicken breast in a large soup pot. Cover with the water, add the salt, and bring to a boil over high heat. Turn down the heat to medium-low and simmer, skimming the foam that rises to the surface every now and then, until the chicken is fully cooked yet still moist, 35 to 40 minutes. Remove the breast from the broth using a pair of tongs and reserve until cool enough to handle. Strain the broth and return it to the pot. Add to the broth the bay leaf, carrots, squash, fava beans, leek, bulgur, and black pepper to taste. Stir to combine and cook over medium heat until the vegetables are tender while still holding their shape and the bulgur puffs up, 20 to 25 minutes.

Meanwhile, shred the chicken breast and transfer to a small bowl. Right before serving, add the lemon zest and juice to the broth. Taste for salt and adjust if needed. Divide the shredded chicken into the soup bowls, ladle in the soup, and garnish with the cilantro.

Ella Schmidt

Chef Ella Schmidt created Maite, a Brooklyn-based restaurant that offers traditional Basque food with a Colombian touch, in 2014. Born in a small municipality in rural Colombia called Victoria (Caldas), Ella moved to the United States with her father when she was fifteen years old. She still remembers climbing up guava trees when she was a child. Back then, the Colombian war was tearing her town apart, so she couldn't easily move around. Even her school was blown up at some point during the conflict.

Her mother and sister have lived in Basque Country, an autonomous region in Spain, for decades. They both work in food as well, hence Ella's predilection for Basque dishes and traditions: a good bottle of wine, small plates to share, and a love for great ham.

A true Colombiana: powerful and fearless.

ODA AL
POSTRE

The Chilean poet Pablo Neruda, known for his transcendent texts on love and life, also wrote odes to tomatoes, watermelons, and onions. One of them concludes:

no pit,
no husk,
no leaves or thorns,
the tomato offers
its gift
of fiery color
and cool completeness.

Far from Neruda's greatness (but motivated by it), my ode is to the closing ceremony of the table ritual. Dessert. That one touch sealing the deal, comforting the heart, and sowing sweet remembrances.

For some, it's a guilty pleasure—I just call it condensed milk. The kind my cousins and I would drink right out of the cans as kids, that we would open ourselves by hitting an old kitchen knife with a river stone at my grandfather's ranch in the Colombian flatlands bordering Venezuela. And dessert can be as simple as that, a spoonful of *arequipe* with figs and cheese or grilled pineapple drizzled with syrup. In this chapter, you will find how traditional ingredients, flavors, history, and preparations inspired my desserts. The *Aplanchados de Helado de Labneh* frozen yogurt recipe, for instance, is how I put together flavors from a dreamy trip to Popayán, or the chocolate, cashew, and tamarind tart evoked by discovering how prolific these nuts are in the Amazon region. Other recipes are tried and true, such as *arequipe* and *enyucado*.

Guava plays a starring role on Colombia's dessert table. This sweet fruit from proliferous trees is found candied or reduced into a jelly paste. Colombian markets will also offer guava pastes wrapped in corn husks—they pair perfectly with cheese. In this chapter you'll find a delicious frozen guava and blackberry cheesecake.

I invite you to relish this A-list of tarts, frozen treats, and cakes, all made with luscious tropical fruits and widely available frozen pulps.

MAKES 1 QUART

For the frozen *labneh*

3 cups *labneh*
(if you don't have labneh, use 3 cups plain 2% Greek yogurt with 3 tablespoons lime juice stirred in)

6 tablespoons Lemon Verbena Syrup (recipe follows)

Sea salt

½ cup frozen passion fruit pulp, thawed and chilled

Lemon Verbena Syrup

½ cup fine white sugar

½ cup water

12 to 15 leaves fresh lemon verbena, plus more for garnish

APLANCHADOS DE HELADO DE LABNEH, MARACUYÁ Y CIDRÓN

PASSION FRUIT & LEMON VERBENA FROZEN LABNEH SANDWICHES

The Middle Eastern yogurt known as *labneh* and its Colombian crème fraîche-like cousin *suero* are a staple in the country's main river valleys: the Sinú and the Magdalena. They were brought over to the region by the Syrian-Lebanese communities and quickly made their way through this river hub into our coast's cuisine. The rich taste of *labneh* can be somewhat replicated with good-quality Greek yogurt (by that I mean at least 2% milkfat) and a few tablespoons of lime juice.

Then there is the lemon verbena, used in medicinal infusions and known to cure everything from chicken pox to broken hearts. Farmers' markets from spring to early fall will have fresh lemon verbena. Fresh laurel leaves are a great substitute; even though the flavor profiles of these two aromatics are different, laurel will infuse an interesting herbaceousness and depth.

These delicious little frozen yogurt sandwiches are made with store-bought puff pastry that is filled with *labneh* and infused lemon verbena syrup to create a tangy, creamy, fragrant dessert. Hopefully you won't need it to cure a broken heart, but just in case...

LEMON VERBENA WITH PASSION FRUIT SWIRL FROZEN LABNEH

I have learned that the key to homemade ice cream or frozen yogurt is to begin with very cold ingredients before pouring them into the machine. This ensures that the mixture freezes quickly—leaving no chance for ice crystals to form—resulting in a creamy texture. If you don't own an ice cream machine, I recommend simply finding a plain frozen yogurt brand that you love (mine are Stonyfield Vanilla Frozen Yogurt and Lifeway Frozen Kefir), letting it soften a bit, and drizzling in the lemon verbena syrup and passion fruit pulp. Stir and refreeze.

For the lemon verbena syrup: Combine the sugar and water in a small saucepan. Take the leaves in the palm of your hand and smack them to release their oils and wonderful aroma. These oils will infuse the syrup and will leave a nice scent on your hands.

For the frozen *labneh*: Stir the *labneh*, lemon verbena syrup, and a pinch of sea salt in a medium bowl. Chill for at least 30 minutes, transfer to an ice cream maker, and churn according to the manufacturer's instructions. Once the frozen yogurt is creamy and set, slowly pour in the passion fruit pulp during the last few turns of the paddle in order to swirl in the juice. It doesn't have to be perfect—the point is to taste bits of passion fruit here and there.

Place the leaves in the sugar water and bring to a boil over high heat until the sugar dissolves. Turn off the heat, cover, and cool. Transfer the syrup to a glass jar and store in the refrigerator for up to 1 month.

For the puff pastry (*aplanchados*)

Preheat the oven to 375°F and line two matching baking sheets with parchment paper. (You will stack these in the oven with the parchment paper sheets in between the dough to keep it from puffing up.)

On a lightly floured surface, roll out one puff pastry sheet to a 12 x 12-inch square.

Place the pastry dough on one of the prepared lined baking sheets, cover with a sheet of parchment paper, and then place the second baking sheet on top. (You are weighing it down so it doesn't puff up.)

Bake for 15 minutes. Carefully remove the top baking sheet and parchment and continue baking until golden brown, 3 to 5 minutes more. (Keep a close eye on the oven, as these turn golden fast.)

Remove from the oven, transfer to a cooling rack, and allow to cool completely.

While the first sheet bakes, roll out the second sheet of puff pastry, repeating the steps above.

To assemble

Evenly spread the softened frozen *labneh* over one of the puff pastry sheets using an off-set spatula. Top with the second sheet and gently press down to sandwich. Place the large sandwich on a baking sheet and freeze for at least 30 minutes or up to 2 hours. Remove from the freezer and cut into 4 strips lengthwise and then 4 strips crosswise, resulting in 16 rectangles (3 x 2 inches). Dust with powdered sugar, garnish with a fresh lemon verbena leaf, and serve.

MAKES 32 FLATS

1-pound box puff pastry sheets, thawed

All-purpose flour, for dusting

Powdered sugar, for dusting

SERVES 4 TO 6

8 ripe but firm, green or black Mission figs, sliced in half lengthwise

5 tablespoons softened mascarpone cheese

5 tablespoons *Arequipe* (recipe follows), *dulce de leche,* or thick caramel

Freshly ground black pepper

Flaky sea salt

Edible flowers, for garnish (optional)

BREVAS CON QUESO Y AREQUIPE

FIGS WITH CHEESE & AREQUIPE

The combination of figs, cheese, and *Arequipe* (page 271) is a sweet-savory blend, brightened with a dash of salt and a touch of spice: an ideal two-bite dessert. This combination comes from the ever-Colombian *brevas,* preserved fruit made with the first harvest of the fig tree, which is dark green, quite astringent, and needs to be cooked in water and sugar to be palatable. Since in the northern hemisphere we are blessed with supple summer figs, I adapted this recipe to combine the best of both worlds.

Place the figs cut side up on a tray. Dollop each half with about 1 teaspoon cheese and drizzle with 1 teaspoon *arequipe.* Season with pepper and salt to taste, garnish with a flower petal, if using, and serve.

TRADITIONAL *AREQUIPE*

16 cups organic whole milk

5 cups sugar

1 teaspoon baking soda

3 cinnamon sticks

1 tablespoon pure
vanilla extract

I have mentioned this velvety caramel several times in the book. *Arequipe* is one of those quintessential flavors in our cuisine. In Colombia *arequipe* is made and combined in various ways. For instance, in the Cauca Valley region, the caramel is bound with rice flour and raisins, then poured into natural gourds, and called *manjar blanco*. *Arequipe* is also layered with guava jelly and packaged into squares, or used as a filling in cakes, pastries, and flans. The "quick" method involves simply boiling sweetened condensed milk right in the can, allowing you to stock your pantry with *arequipe* at the ready anytime you need it.

Pour the milk into a wide heavy-bottom pot. Stir in the sugar, baking soda, and cinnamon sticks. Cook over medium-high heat until right before it comes to a boil, then quickly lower the heat and simmer for 1 hour and 30 minutes, stirring now and then. Once the milk begins to caramelize and thicken, stir more often, until thick and creamy, about 3½ hours. Stir in the vanilla extract, remove from the heat, and allow to cool completely before using.

QUICK AREQUIPE

MAKES 2 CANS WORTH

2 (14-ounce) cans sweetened
condensed milk, labels
removed

Place the cans in a large pot, and cover completely with water. Bring the water to a boil, then reduce the heat to a steady simmer and cook for 3 hours. Carefully lift the cans from the water and allow them to cool completely before opening.

SERVES 8 TO 12

¼ cup melted unsalted butter, plus more for greasing the mold

32 ounces frozen grated yuca, thawed*

8 ounces ground *costeño* or Cotija cheese

8 ounces grated fresh or frozen coconut (if frozen, thawed)

1 teaspoon anise seeds

1 cup sweetened condensed milk

ENYUCADO

YUCA CAKE

The best *enyucado* I ever tasted was in a little neighborhood bakery owned by Elsie Figueroa, a Cartagenian woman who began making desserts for sale in her home to support her family. She managed to turn her hobby into a successful business and, some twenty years later, her daughters Vanessa and Paola run one of the most beautiful dessert companies in the city. They have become my go-to advisers for desserts. Full disclosure: the sisters gifted Diego and me with our unforgettable wedding cake.

Especially easy to make, this simple cake has a pleasant gummy texture and toasty corners. It isn't too sweet, and it can be served warm with a scoop of vanilla ice cream.

Preheat the oven to 375°F.

Grease a 9 x 13-inch baking pan or a 12-cup Bundt cake pan with butter.

Stir together the yuca, cheese, coconut, butter, and anise seeds. Fold in the sweetened condensed milk. Transfer the mixture to the prepared baking pan and spread evenly with the back of a spoon.

Bake until set and light golden brown, 35 to 40 minutes.

Allow to cool and serve warm or at room temperature.

***Note:** I recommend buying frozen grated yuca and coconut. These can usually be found in the grocery store's frozen section, near the vegetables. My go-to brand is La Fe Foods.

**MAKES 44 COOKIES
(2½-INCH DIAMETER) OR
22 COOKIE SANDWICHES**

½ cup barley flour

2½ cups all-purpose flour,
plus more for dusting

¼ teaspoon baking powder

1 teaspoon kosher salt

1 cup unsalted butter,
softened

¾ cup granulated sugar

1 vanilla pod, seeds scraped
and set aside

1 egg

½ cup apricot jam
(or any of your favorite jams)

Powdered sugar

GALLETITAS DE CEBADA TOSTADA Y MERMELADA

TOASTED BARLEY & JAM COOKIES

Linzer cookies, brought to us courtesy of a small town in Austria called Linz, are an influence in pastries and shortcake-making that traveled all the way to the small town of Tinjacá and took hold. My take involves toasting the barley flour, local to the region, until nutty brown, and adding a dollop of jam. My favorite is bitter orange, but please do get creative with any tropical jam you might encounter in farmers' markets and specialty markets: mango, *uchuva* (husk cherry), or passion fruit. The world is your... choice of jam!

Preheat the oven to 350°F. Line four baking sheets with parchment paper. (Have 2 round cookie cutters at hand, 2½-inch and 1-inch diameter.)

Heat a dry medium skillet over medium-low heat. Add the barley flour and swirl it in the pan—you can also use a wooden spoon to move the flour around—until toasted, 3 to 5 minutes, and you can smell the nutty scent. Make sure the flour doesn't burn. When properly toasted, the flour will take on a pale beige color. Remove from the heat and cool.

Sift together the toasted barley flour, all-purpose flour, and baking powder into a bowl. Stir in the salt.

In the bowl of a stand mixer with the paddle attachment, whip the butter until creamy and pale yellow. Add the granulated sugar and beat for 1 to 2 minutes, until the sugar crystals have dissolved. Add the vanilla seeds and egg and continue whisking fully incorporated, stopping to scrape the sides of the bowl if necessary.

Add the dry ingredients to the butter, 1 cup at a time, and mix a few turns on low speed to incorporate—do not overmix. Blend until the dough comes together.

Remove the dough from the mixer, cover with plastic wrap, and allow to rest for 10 to 20 minutes.

Bring the dough together, divide it in half, and form two flattened discs. Cover the discs with plastic wrap and chill for 20 minutes in the fridge. (This makes for a perfect clean cut.)

Dust a clean countertop with flour. Remove one of the discs from the fridge and roll out the dough using a rolling pin, until the dough is about ⅛-inch thick. Using a round cookie cutter (2½-inch diameter), cut rounds from the dough and place on the prepared baking sheet. Repeat this process until you use all the dough. (You might have to use two baking sheets. You should have around 22 raw cookies.) Place the tray(s) in the fridge and remove the second disc from the fridge. Dust the countertop with more flour and roll out the dough, repeating the instructions above. For the second disc, use the same cookie cutter to cut out the cookies. Before you place the raw cookies on the prepared tray, use the 1-inch cookie cutter to cut "holes" out of the center of each cookie-dough round, and place the cut cookie dough on the prepared baking sheet(s). You might have to use two baking sheets.

Remove the baking sheet with chilled cookies from the fridge and replace it with the second tray of cookies. Bake the chilled cookies for 8 to 10 minutes, until the cookies are slightly brown on the edges. (Make sure you switch trays from top to bottom to ensure even baking.) Remove from the oven and let cool completely on a cookie rack.

Meanwhile, bake the second batch of cookies, repeating the same process.

After all the cookies have cooled, place 1 teaspoon jam in the center of each cookie round—the ones without the hole. Spread the jam with an offset spatula or butter knife and place a cookie with a hole on top to create a cookie sandwich. Repeat until all the cookies are assembled. Dust with powdered sugar. These cookies keep well for 5 to 7 days in an airtight container.

HELADO DE MILO Y BANANOS CARAMELIZADOS

MILO ICE CREAM WITH CARAMELIZED BANANAS

MAKES 1 PINT

2 pasteurized eggs

½ cup sugar

½ cup Milo

½ cup heavy cream

2 cups fresh milk

½ cup powdered milk

1 teaspoon sea salt

For the caramelized bananas

3 large medium-ripe bananas

3 tablespoons sugar

"Milo gives you strength, you set the goal," reads the slogan for a Colombian granulated chocolate drink. I grew up obsessed with its chocolaty and crunchy texture. Definitely the breakfast drink of my childhood.

I'd drink it dissolved in a glass of milk almost every morning before school, and on the weekends, it would be prepared in the blender with ice, like a milk-shake. This ice cream version is meant to be prepared with Milo, which is very common at Asian, West Indian, Caribbean, and Latin American markets, but feel free to replace with any other chocolate drink mix of your choice.

Whisk the eggs and sugar in a bowl until the mixture becomes pale yellow and ribbony. Add the Milo and whisk to incorporate. In a separate bowl, whisk the heavy cream, fresh milk, and powdered milk together until the powdered milk has dissolved. Pour into the egg and Milo mixture and stir to incorporate. Refrigerate until very cold, 20 to 30 minutes. Transfer to an ice cream machine and freeze following the manufacturer's instructions.

CARAMELIZED BANANAS

Preheat the broiler to high.

Cut the bananas on the bias into ¼-inch-thick slices. Place on a baking sheet. Sprinkle with the sugar and place under the broiler until golden and bubbly, 2 to 3 minutes. Watch closely to make sure the sugar does not burn.

Scoop the ice cream into bowls, top with the caramelized bananas, and serve.

SERVES 6 TO 8

For the cake roll

Nonstick cooking spray

5 large organic eggs, at room temperature, yolks and whites separated

1 cup sugar, divided

2 teaspoons pure vanilla extract

¼ teaspoon kosher salt

¾ cup all-purpose flour, sifted

½ teaspoon cream of tartar

½ cup raspberry powder (for color)

For the filling

½ cup mascarpone or cream cheese, softened at room temperature

½ cup Quick *Arequipe*, at room temperature (page 271), or store-bought

¼ cup raspberry jam

LIBERAL DE AREQUIPE Y FRAMBUESAS

RASPBERRY ROLL CAKE WITH AREQUIPE

The liberal is a bright pinkish/reddish roll cake. Its color and name go back to a time of civil war and the birth of the country's infamous conflict.

In the early twentieth century, Colombia's two main political parties were involved in constant violent clashes for power across the country, each with a distinct color: the conservatives were blue and the liberals were red, hence the traditional name of this pastry. In time, these two parties lost their influence on multiple options in the country's political spectrum, but the legendary cake still remains a central treat at Colombia's roadside stands and small-town bakeries.

I'll always remember watching my husband, Diego, gleefully taking a bite out of a bright red liberal at a *tienda* (bodega) in the Candelaria neighborhood of Bogotá. It's a memory I cherish. This one's for you.

Preheat the oven to 350°F. Grease a 15 x 10-inch baking sheet with cooking spray and line with parchment paper. Cut the parchment paper with a bit of an overhang on each long end for easy lifting. Spray the parchment as well.

In a large bowl, beat the egg yolks with an electric mixer until thickened. Gradually add ½ cup of the sugar and beat until thick, pale yellow ribbons form, 3 to 4 minutes. Pour in the vanilla extract and continue mixing for a few seconds to incorporate. Using a rubber spatula, fold in the flour. Set aside.

Place the egg whites and cream of tartar in a separate bowl. With clean beaters, whisk, slowly increasing the speed, until soft peaks form. Gradually add the remaining ½ cup sugar, 1 tablespoon at a time. Make sure you incorporate each tablespoon fully before adding the next.

Fold one-third of the whites into the reserved flour and egg mixture until fully incorporated to loosen the batter and make it easier to fold in the remaining whites without having to stir too much (which would deflate the batter).

Spread the mixture evenly onto the prepared baking sheet. Bake in the preheated oven until the cake is light golden brown and pulls from the sides of the pan, 12 to 15 minutes.

While the cake bakes, place the raspberry powder in a small fine-mesh sieve. Lay a kitchen towel flat and generously dust with the berry powder. This berry-dusted towel is what you'll use to roll up the cake so it doesn't stick onto itself.

Make the filling: In a small bowl, combine the mascarpone and *arequipe* using a spatula. Set aside.

Remove the cake from the oven and let cool for 5 minutes. Invert onto the towel dusted with the raspberry powder. Carefully peel off all the parchment paper and roll the cake in the towel as you would a jelly roll, starting from the short side.

Allow the roll to cool completely on a wire rack.

Assemble the liberal by unrolling the cake and spread the raspberry jelly evenly from corner to corner with an offset spatula or butter knife. Spread the *arequipe* and mascarpone mixture over the jam, leaving about a 1-inch border so that the filling doesn't ooze out. Roll up the cake again, this time without the towel. Transfer to a tray, seam side down, and refrigerate until cold. Dust with a bit more raspberry powder to even out the color, then slice and serve.

**SERVES 6 TO 8
(7 CUPS)**

1 cup white rice

4 cups water

2 cinnamon sticks

3 teaspoons cinnamon

½ teaspoon nutmeg

8 to 10 whole cloves,
mashed in a mortar

3 cups whole milk

2 cups unsweetened
dried coconut

1 cup heavy cream

1 (14.5-ounce) can
sweetened condensed
milk

1 tablespoon aged rum
(optional)

Kosher salt

ARROZ "COCADA"

CARAMELIZED COCONUT RICE PUDDING

Are there too many rice pudding recipes out there? Is it necessary to develop yet another? As I pondered these questions, my friend Paola, who lives in Hong Kong and is an extraordinary cook, asked if I was making an arroz con leche for the book. I then thought: If a Colombiana like her, who has lived all over the world, immediately thinks of rice pudding as a must, there is no reason for me not to do the same.

In a large heavy-bottom saucepan, combine the rice, water, cinnamon sticks, ground cinnamon, nutmeg, and cloves. Cook over medium-high heat until it comes to a boil. Turn the heat down to medium and simmer, stirring every 3 minutes or so with a wooden spoon, until the rice is close to being completely cooked and has absorbed most of the water, about 15 minutes.

Add the whole milk and coconut and cook over medium-high heat until the mixture comes to a boil. Lower the heat to medium and simmer for 5 to 7 minutes, stirring with a wooden spoon.

Add the heavy cream, condensed milk, rum, if using, and a generous pinch of salt and cook over medium-high heat until the mixture comes to a boil. Lower the heat to medium and simmer for 3 to 5 minutes. Turn off the heat.

Serve warm or cold. The rice pudding keeps, refrigerated, for up to 5 days in a tightly sealed container in the refrigerator.

MAKES 6 ICE POPS

2½ cups whole milk

½ cup water

½ cup quick-cooking oats

1 cinnamon stick

1 teaspoon ground cinnamon

¼ teaspoon ground cloves

⅓ cup ground panela,
brown sugar, or coconut sugar

1 teaspoon vanilla extract

Kosher salt

PALETAS DE AVENA Y CANELA

OAT & CINNAMON ICE CREAM BARS

In the town of Espinal, it's customary to go out to the square at night, when the air is cooler. People enjoy *avena helada*, a very cold, milky oat drink, similar to Mexican *horchata*. The *avena* flows all night, served from humongous aluminum pots with large chunks of ice and floating cinnamon sticks in street vendors' carts. They also enjoy plenty of *aguardiente* and beer, dancing the night away (some barefoot, some in their flip-flops).

These ice pops are inspired by this drink and their creaminess is transportive.

In a medium heavy saucepan, heat the milk, water, oats, cinnamon stick, ground cinnamon. cloves, *panela*, vanilla extract, and a generous pinch of salt over medium-low heat for 8 to 10 minutes, until the mixture reaches a simmer, then turn the heat down to low. Do not allow the mixture to boil, as it may overflow.

Simmer over low heat for 8 to 10 minutes, until the mixture starts to thicken. Make sure you stir often with a wooden spoon to avoid the mixture sticking to the bottom of the saucepan.

Remove the saucepan from the heat and let the mixture cool for 20 to 30 minutes.

Using kitchen tongs, remove the cinnamon stick from the mixture and discard.

Divide the cooled mixture into 6 ice pop molds using ½ cup per mold. Insert ice pop sticks and freeze for 7 hours minimum.

SERVES 6 TO 8

2 small ripe pineapples, peeled and cut into ¼-inch-thick rounds

1 tablespoon unsalted butter, melted

½ cup Elderberry Cordial (recipe follows) or store-bought Elderflower Syrup by Belvoir

1 cup crème fraîche or plain Greek yogurt

PIÑA ASADA CON ALMÍBAR DE SAUCO

CHARRED PINEAPPLE WITH ELDERBERRY SYRUP

Elderberry trees grow all over the high-altitude areas of the Andes. Their tiny white flowers will bloom and then fall, blanketing the grasses of cold-weather parks and fields.

Often used for medicinal purposes like cough drops, these flowers have a subtle tangy taste and are quite delicious. The flower's syrup and the grilled pineapple's dark char makes this dessert a sophisticated end to any meal. The sweet, bitter, and floral blend can be rounded out with a dollop of crème fraîche.

Make sure you buy very ripe pineapples. The trick to knowing if they are ready is to pull off a leaf from the center of the top—if it comes out easily, it is ready. Also, trust your sense of smell. The citrusy aroma is always a reliable guide.

Prepare the grill for high heat. Place the pineapple rounds on a parchment paper–lined baking sheet. Brush the pineapple with the melted butter and drizzle with ¼ cup of the elderberry cordial.

Cook on the prepared grill for about 4 minutes per side, until golden brown and charred in places. The char adds an interesting layer of texture and bitter flavor to the fruit.

Transfer to a platter and drizzle with the remaining ¼ cup elderberry cordial, and serve the crème fraîche alongside.

ELDERBERRY CORDIAL

½ cup fine white sugar

½ cup water

2 tablespoons dried elderberries or juniper berries

Combine the sugar and water in a small saucepan. Place the berries in the sugar water and bring to a boil over high heat; cook until the sugar dissolves. Turn off the heat, cover, and leave on the stove until cool. Transfer to a glass jar and store in the refrigerator for up to 1 month.

MAKES ONE 10-INCH TART

10-inch fluted tart pan with removable bottom or a rectangular 14 x 5-inch fluted tart pan with removable bottom

For the crust

¾ cup raw cashews

¾ cup buckwheat flour

⅓ cup coconut oil

¼ cup ground panela or brown sugar

Kosher salt

For the filling

8 ounces 70% dark chocolate, chopped

⅓ cup ground panela or light brown sugar

1 cup whole-milk Greek yogurt, chilled

½ cup tamarind concentrate or paste (seeds removed)

1½ cups heavy cream

¼ cup toasted cashews

Flaky sea salt

TARTALETA DE CHOCOLATE, TAMARINDO Y MARAÑÓN

CHOCOLATE, TAMARIND & CASHEW TART

I have been making variations of these dark chocolate tarts for many years, varying the crust, the fats, and the filling. This one slices particularly well, and it has an elegant sweetness. Tamarind concentrate can be found in the Asian section of the grocery store and it comes in syrup form.

Preheat the oven to 375°F.

Make the crust: Place the cashews and flour in the bowl of a food processor, and pulse until cashews are broken into smaller pieces. Add the coconut oil, *panela*, and a pinch of salt, and pulse a few more times until the dough comes together. Transfer the dough to the tart pan and press down with your fingers, evenly forming a crust on the bottom and sides. Freeze for 20 minutes.

Place the tart crust on a sheet pan and bake until light golden brown, 8 to 10 minutes. Allow to cool completely on a baking rack.

Prepare the filling: Place the chocolate and *panela* in a non-reactive heatproof bowl. Set over a small pot of boiling water and cook, stirring often to incorporate, until the *panela* has dissolved and the chocolate is melted.

Remove the bowl from the heat and let the mixture cool. In a separate bowl, whisk together the yogurt and tamarind concentrate. Fold in the melted chocolate. Pour the filling into the cooled crust and chill in the refrigerator until the tart is set, 50 minutes to 1 hour.

Meanwhile, place the metal bowl of the stand mixer and whisk attachment in the freezer for at least 10 minutes. Chilling the bowl and the whisk to whip the cream shortens the process and prevents the cream from turning into butter from overmixing.

Remove the chilled bowl and whisk from the freezer, pour in the cream, and whisk until soft peaks form. Transfer the whipped cream to a separate bowl and refrigerate.

Right before serving, remove the tart from the refrigerator, sprinkle with the toasted cashews and salt, and serve with the whipped cream on the side.

ODA AL POSTRE

For the crust

7 ounces round tea biscuits (200-gram package roll), popularly known as Maria cookies or Maria biscuits, or substitute graham crackers

4 tablespoons unsalted butter, melted

1 teaspoon ground cardamom

For the topping

1 pound small guavas, peeled, halved, and seeded

3 cups fresh blackberries

2 tablespoons sugar

1 tablespoon water

2 tablespoons sherry

For the filling

2 (8-ounce) packages of cream cheese, at room temperature

1 cup 2% plain Greek yogurt, chilled

1 cup sweetened condensed milk

1 teaspoon kosher salt

½ cup *arequipe* (page 271) or dulce de leche

TORTA HELADA DE GUAYABA, AREQUIPE & MORAS

FROZEN GUAVA & BLACKBERRY CHEESECAKE

A quite common snack is a slab of guava paste stacked over a slice of white cheese and a spoonful of *arequipe*—the perfect bite, indeed.

Most airport food stores in Colombia offer tiny, portable versions of this dessert. Sometimes, you can even find a bite-size white cheese with the *arequipe* or guava paste already inside, gently oozing out after the first bite. My take on this ubiquitous flavor combination is rather delicate and less sweet.

Remove the guava seeds, using a teaspoon measure or a melon baller to swiftly scoop the seeded center out, leaving the shells hollow. Keep in mind, this recipe can be made a day or two ahead, which means you'll have one less thing to do when you're entertaining!

Preheat the oven to 400°F.

Grease and line a 9-inch springform cake pan with parchment paper. Line a baking sheet with parchment paper.

Make the crust: Place the biscuits in the food processor and grind to form very fine crumbs. Transfer to a bowl and stir in the melted butter and cardamom. Using your hands, press the crust onto the bottom of the prepared pan and use the back of a spoon to even out the dough. Freeze for 20 to 25 minutes.

Make the topping: Place the guava halves and blackberries in a large metal bowl. Sprinkle with the sugar, water, and sherry and toss to coat. Place the guava, cut side down, and the blackberries on the prepared baking sheet and bake until the fruit begins to brown, burst, and soften, while still holding its shape, 20 to 25 minutes.

Make the filling: Place the cream cheese in the bowl of a stand mixer and beat with the paddle attachment until light and airy, 3 to 4 minutes. Pour in the yogurt and sweetened condensed milk and add the salt. Continue mixing to obtain a velvety and airy mixture, about 4 minutes.

Using an offset spatula or butter knife, spread the *arequipe* evenly over the cookie crust layer that is now fully set. Place half of the guava halves (cut side down) and half of the berries on the *arequipe*. Reserve the remaining guava and blackberries for serving. Gently pour the cream cheese filling over the roasted fruit, smoothing the top. Transfer to the freezer until set, 1 hour to 1 hour 30 minutes.

Before serving, remove the outer ring of the springform pan, slide the tart onto a pretty cake stand, and garnish with the reserved roasted fruit and their juices. Slice into wedges and serve.

Aura Salcedo

Aura has always gravitated toward big cities, so her hometown of Montería (Cordoba), on Colombia's northern coast, soon became too small for this talented cook. Aura left in her early twenties and taught herself how to cook while cleaning houses in Cartagena, the country's most visited city. In between her usual tasks, she would peek into the kitchen to learn processes and tips while watching the cooking staff in action. She would take these lessons and explore them further with her family, cooking meals for her mother, two brothers, and three sisters.

Aura then took her knowledge from Colombia to family homes in Panama; Las Vegas, Nevada; and, most recently, New York City. Wherever she goes, she takes Colombian cuisine with her, along with the memories of early years spent in long conversations and laughter with family and neighbors on the front porch.

When the 2020 pandemic took away her job as a cleaner at a Times Square hotel, Aura used this time to focus on her cooking skills, not only sharing her ideas and talent with her Mexican roommate but also collaborating with Mariana in the making of this book.

AUTHOR'S NOTE

This manuscript was submitted to HarperCollins on April 7, 2020, during the first COVID-19 lockdown, from our home in South Williamsburg in Brooklyn, New York. More than ever, cooking has become a source of comfort and care. Learning to cope with uncertainty suddenly gave me the courage to write from a more personal place. Seclusion even inspired my husband, Diego, to cook by following recipes for the first time! A newly found appreciation for the essential beauty and gifts of everyday life illuminates these pages.

The vision of going on a ten-day road trip from Bogotá to Cartagena to photograph the places, food, and people transformed into shooting the book entirely in Brooklyn due to the pandemic. Creative challenges can bring unexpected results.

It is my wish that these recipes give you as much comfort and joy as they gave us. Hopefully in brighter times.

Mariana

ACKNOWLEDGMENTS

To Liz Moody, who on an early summer night, at the bar of a Fort Greene restaurant, asked me why I hadn't written a Colombian cookbook yet. Liz, you pushed me to do something I didn't even know I wanted so much.

My agents, Anna Worrall and Alia Hanna Habib at Gernert, you two saw this project, believed in it from the start, and accompanied me and cheered me on every step of the way. Thank you.

To Julie Will, my editor, who took my words and made them flourish. Your perspective made me look at the work in different ways and enticed me to explore cultural and historical references in a deeper sense. Emma Kupor, your sharp eye and awareness helped me see so many nuances about my culture's perception that needed revisiting. Thank you.

Andrea Gentl and Martin Hyers, the very first shot was the *caldo de costilla*, and the very last the coconut kaffir dessert. From beginning to end, you gave light, magic, and a sense of place to every image. This collaboration surpassed everything I had dreamed the book to be. I cannot wait for us to go to Colombia together.

To the crew: Francesca Critchton, Sam Mackenzie, Anahita Tajmaher, Peisin Yang Lazo, Jezz Hill, and Aura Salcedo, your hard work, commitment, and resilience through the hottest days of summer made this project a dream.

Diego, there wasn't a line in this book you didn't read. I couldn't have done the project without your eyes and brilliance. You helped me put my vision on paper and made the prose flow. Thank you for your patience, love, and for making the Liberal your own.

To Michelle Perez, who not only designed my book proposal but gave me light when I was doubtful. Along with your husband, Victor Hugo, you tasted, critiqued, and celebrated many recipes in this book. More is more. Mepe Carrizosa, your beautifully illustrated map placed our country with all of its abundance and beauty.

Gracias a las Colombianas!! Gaeleen Quinn, Viviana Lewis, Aura Salsedo, La Nena Sierra, Ella Schmidt, Carolina Peña for telling your stories, for keeping our cuisine alive and thriving away from home . . .

Lauren Volo, whose brilliant light and friendship made this project possible from the start. Thank you.

Thanks to Tarajia Morrell for guiding and encouraging me to be authentic, from the pile of napkins after a big party to turning mossy garden steps into an *aperitivo* bar.

Deep gratitude to Ken Holzberg and Tom Kopfensteiner of Stonewood Farms for such a generous invitation and allowing us to photograph on your dream farm.

Thanks to Howard Bellin for your magical garden!

Jose Lloreda (Orocosta-Tropicals), thanks to your gorgeous exuberant leaves, anthuriums, ginger flowers, and foliage, we brought the tropics to these pages. Receiving that box of nature's beauty was a wonderful gift.

To Cathy and Peter Morrell, thank you for making us feel at home.

Natalia Gaviria, who tirelessly cooked, tested, tasted, and adjusted recipes with me. Without your formidable feedback and infinite and honest friendship, I wouldn't be here. Gracias.

Mami, Billy, y Cami por el tiempo, el cariño, los momentos compartidos, y por supuesto el milo de cada mañana y los *Sancochos* en Peñalisa.

A mi Papá, Camilo Velásquez Turbay, por compartir tantas historias, preparaciones, experiencias, y el sabor de su tierra conmigo.

A mis tías y mis primas quienes son mujeres fabulosas, fuertes, y amorosas.

Maria Helena, Octavio y Estefanía, infinitas gracias por todo su apoyo y respaldo a travez de los años. Así mismo a Connie por tu cariño y paciencia.

To Mono and Marea, my partners in crime, together we make a dream team and I cannot wait to continue to collaborate.

Diego Patiño, for sitting at our table, tasting, confiding, and sharing our New York life with us.

Fernando Aciar, Anna Polonsky, Gaeleen Quinn, Pablo Goldberg, Miguel Posada, Christelle Michellet, Carlos Julio Mesa, Jennifer Rose Parker, Adam Kimmel, Simon Lewis, and Jan Schollenberger, thank you for the feedback, the dinner parties, tasting recipes, and being in our family.

Arthur Fournier, you showed me a way to expand the visual narrative of these pages. Thank you for reaching out to your network of librarians and scholars around the world and helping me find the beauty of archival images.

So much gratitude and appreciation for the parts you all played in this book: Michael Harland Turkell, Heritage Radio Network, Yael Raviv, and Emilie Baltz.

Thanks to chef Craig Von Foerster, for opening the doors of your kitchen and showing me my dream of cooking was possible. To Heather Foster, for taking me under your wing and becoming a lifelong friend. To Lane Rowland, for teaching me about the philosophy of cooking, life, and love.

Maria Cristina Toro, your love, trust, and support gave me a career.

To Debbie Peterson, for a friendship built in -30°F weather, for a drive across the country eating grilled cheese sandwiches and oranges, and for making me taste your velouté dozens of times.

To Molly Stevens, for teaching me that well-written recipes should be a joy to read.

Paula Mendoza, for awakening my innate passion and love for fashion and style. For carefully curating some of the clothes I wore throughout the making of this book and for standing by my side.

Alicia Mejia, for sharing her knowledge about identity and culture. Kelly Talamas and Cristina Cabarcos—thank you for your generosity, and I celebrate your adopted Colombianity.

To Katherine W. Robinson, for your friendship and support.

Immense gratitude to my friends and partners in crime, wine, travels, love, and dreams: Paola Victoria, Laura Saenz, Mariana Suarez, Fryda Baum, Ana Laura Vargas, Mepe Carrizosa, Ana Maria Palacios, Manuela Zuluaga, Irina Khasternova, Carolina Rubio-MacWright, and Melissa Pinto.

Paola Sinisterra, Kate Jones, and Cathy Chon, for showing me and welcoming me into a world of exquisite beauty, food, style, and grit. Thank you.

A Beatriz Restrepo. Tu sabes . . .

Javier Uribe, por una amistad infinita, por tu barra, tu apoyo, por hacerme reír y por supuesto aquel sancocho de gallina criolla en la Vega.

To Lizzie Eder and Jaime Zobel, for opening the doors of Don Benito and for inspiring the Winds of la Heróica Feast.

Adriana Meluk and Elise Gold, for guiding me and keeping me connected to myself throughout this journey.

To my food styling mentors, Jee Levin and Allison Attenborough.

To Zach Kleinman, for helping me trust every scoop, to stay local, and to slow down.

Gracias a mis amigas de infancia: Nana Montenegro, Tacha Uribe, Ale Quintero, Ana Laverde, Juana de la Vega, Yaya Prieto, Ana Galindo, Caro Uribe, y Cata Salazar.

A la Reina de las Nieves.

Gracias to the Makers

Every piece of fabric and tableware, every spoon, dress, and platter made it to the set for a reason. A group of makers, designers, and artists gave life to the images, and their work and craft was a powerful source of inspiration. Thank you.

Cristina Grajales—with Jorge Lizarazo's Hechizoo
DBO HOME— Dana Brandwein
Plaza Bolivar—Mariana Suárez
Melissa Goldstein By Hand
Francisco Leal y Karen Daccarett
Olga Piedrahita—Danielle La Fourie
Johanna Ortiz
Paula Mendoza, Looking for the Masters
Silvia Tcherassi
Maison Alma
Cerámicas El Dorado Carmen de Viboral
Prop Haus—Martha Bernabe
Prop Workshop
99 Scott

BIBLIOGRAPHY

Díaz Piedrahita, Santiago. *Las Hojas de Las Plantas Como Envoltura de Alimentos.* Ministerio de Cultura. Published between 1975 and 1977.

Garcia, Lorena. *Lorena Garcia's New Taco Classics.* Celebra, 2015.

García Usta, Jorge. *Árabes en Macondo.* El Ancora Editores, 2015.

German, Patiño, Julián Estrada, Estrella De Los Ríos, and Maria Yances. *Colombia Cocina de Regiones.* MNR Ediciones, 2013.

Hoyos, Cristo. *Tambucos, ceretas y cafongos: Recipientes, soportes y empaques del antiguo departamento de Bolívar.* Ministerio de Cultura, 2012.

Malgieri, Nick. *Perfect Cakes.* HarperCollins, 2002.

Ordóñez Caicedo, Carlos. *Gran Libro de la Cocina Colombiana.* Instituto Colombiana de Cultura, 1991.

Ospina de Navarro, Sofia. *La Cartilla del Hogar.* Editorial Granamerica, 1967.

Román de Zurek, Teresita. *Cartagena de Indias en La Olla.* Gamma Ediciones, 2000.

———. *Cartagena de Indias en La Olla—Las Mejores 200 Recetas.* Gamma Ediciones, 2000.

Stevens, Molly. *All About Braising.* W. W. Norton, 2004.

Velásquez, Mariana. *Frutas, Cocina Inspirada en Sabores Tropicales.* Gamma Ediciones, 2011.

Villegas, Benjamin. *El Sabor de Colombia.* Villegas Editores, 1994.

Villegas, Liliana. *Deliciosas Frutas Tropicales.* Villegas Editores, 2001.

Electronic Sources

Tribulaciones Sobre la Arepa by Julian Estrada

Universo Centro

www.universocentro.com/NUMERO31/Tribulacionessobrelaarepa.aspx

El Condimentario

www.elcondimentariodemargarita.com/category/historia-y-literatura/antojos-literarios/

My Colombian Recipes

www.mycolombianrecipes.com/

Colombian Ministry of Culture

www.mincultura.gov.co/areas/patrimonio/Paginas/bibliotecas-de-cocinas.aspx

INDEX

ABOUT THE AUTHOR

Mariana Velásquez is an award-winning international food stylist and chef. Her work has been featured in the *New York Times*, *Vogue*, *Food & Wine*, *Bon Appétit*, and *Gourmet*, to name a few. A published author of three recipe books, she has also styled, art-directed, developed recipes for, and collaborated on more than twenty cookbooks throughout her career, including James Beard Award winners. She has received attention from former First Lady Michelle Obama, who hired Mariana to food-style the First Lady's American Grown project. Born in Bogotá, Mariana lives in Brooklyn, New York, with her husband.